SIT DOWN!
SPEAK UP!
CASH IN!

A CEO's Guide to Peer Advisory Groups

TINA CORNER

LXCouncil, Inc.
www.lxcouncil.com
Phone: 410-970-4771

Published by LXCouncil, Inc.:
07/2019

ISBN: 978-1-0830409-2-3

Book cover design by: Barbara Buren 2019

To my dad for being my hero and role model on what it takes to be an entrepreneur. You are missed greatly.

CONTENTS

If you build it…

If you build it, they will come is a dream that only comes true on the silver screen. By the same token, you can keep on doing what you've always done and expect different results, but it's unlikely that will happen, either. Albert Einstein said it best: "The definition of insanity: doing the same thing over and over again and expecting different results." Or you can reap the benefits of having a team with the experience and solutions that will take you to the top. If you're a CEO, business owner, or entrepreneur who really wants to build a wildly successful business, you need more than a dream—you need a dream team.

Sit Down! Speak Up! Cash In! is about how thousands of CEOs sit down every month with their peers and speak up to share their insights, perspectives, and experiences as owners. As a result, they cash in on the epiphanies, ideas, and solutions that propel their business forward faster than forging alone. This book is about the best-kept secret in business—peer advisory councils. A peer advisory council consists of peers, in this case, owners and presidents, who act as each other's board of advisors without fiduciary responsibility.

Think about what a peer advisory council really is. The concept isn't new, but the reality remains that many highly successful people in business don't avail themselves of the benefits that these groups can offer. As noted, a peer advisory group is your dream team! Who else are you going to talk to that has unbiased feedback, different perspectives, and solutions you never considered? In this book, I'll share stories about people who have experienced uncertainty, struggles, and challenges in their day-to-day business operations, and I'll reveal how they used peer advisory councils to overcome them.

This book will show you how you can benefit from a dream team of your own. You'll learn what a peer advisory council is, what the benefits are such as not feeling alone at the top, and what you don't know you don't know or have forgotten! I will show you how you can become involved and take advantage of this little-known, but very effective, business resource. You'll learn the who, what, where, and when of peer advisory councils, but first and foremost, you'll discover the why.

I've created, developed, and moderated over three hundred unique peer-to-peer advisory council meetings and have spent nearly ten thousand hours in this process. When I first learned about what peer groups do and how they work, I became excited because the basic concept of smart people getting together to share their knowledge with each other simply makes good business sense. As the expression goes, two heads are better than one. So, it stands to reason that half a dozen or more intelligent businesspeople would be even better!

I've taken my experience and created a company with a proven, unique peer advisory model. The model addresses the areas in the industry that create a less-than-stellar experience for the member, like less than full boards of advisors, the wrong peers matched with each other, and poor moderating/facilitating. The reason I have devoted the last eight years of my life to this is because I'm a business owner too. I know what it is like to feel lonely at the top and wonder if you are making the right decision or have the right focus for the now. I am all too aware of how it feels to put it all on the line. I have walked in your shoes and know that the path is often bumpy, with no road map to guide you in the right direction. And I also know there is nothing more rewarding.

I spent many of my early years in the corporate world, at one point running a $1.2 billion division for a global corporation. Raised by an entrepreneur, it was not my intent to follow the same path. In fact, I thought the corporate life was my answer. I considered corporate structure to be safe compared to my dad, who always had unpredictability with his businesses. Cash flow was not steady, and the economy created challenges for the work he was in. Corporate life provided a game plan that if followed well, you advanced. Not much

risk; I never risked "my" money. It was always the company's money. It's like gambling with a safety net. I only realized later in life that my father was an entrepreneur and he made a big impression on both me and my natural acclimation toward small businesses. Over the years, he had a diverse range of businesses in the Midwest and had both predictability and more control and freedom than I did with a large company. That was a revelation.

Why, you ask, join a peer advisory council? Because you've tried everything else, but nothing seems to work exactly right or it takes too long; because you don't have all the answers; because you need a "secret weapon" that's proven to be effective; but, mainly, because you can't afford not to, especially in today's difficult economic climate. Independent business owners have too much at risk to not give themselves every opportunity to build the very best company possible while becoming the very best leader they can be!

Inertia is your enemy. Business owners know it's never an option to sit still and do nothing, because nothing means that—nothing. In essence, it means stagnation, malaise, and ultimately, failure. Nothing ever stays the same. Either momentum will move you forward, or a lack of momentum will move you backward. Ask yourself this question: at this very moment, which direction is your company moving? If it is forward, is it at the rate you expect or want and desire? Or is it backward, and what will happen if you let this backward direction continue? You have to ask yourself, "Do I want to change the direction I'm going and change the inevitable result?" If you do, a peer advisory council can help you.

I chose a career in sales after working for my father whenever

I came home in the summers during college. I quickly learned that there is an enormous lack of formal resources for those who count on sales to make a living. In fact, there is no such thing as a college sales degree. I did complete a salesmanship class at the University of Missouri, but barely skated by—my answers were not what the instructor wanted. My answers were based on the real world of business and my experience watching my father successfully run and sell his businesses.

As an example, Dad was always on his cell phone working the sale. On one particular day when he was visiting me in Annapolis, we were driving when his phone rang. I could immediately tell from his side of the conversation that this was someone who wanted to buy one of Dad's used concrete mixer trucks. He listened quietly while the man on the other end pleaded his case for why the price of the truck should be $34,000, instead of $38,000, Dad's asking price. After listening for a few minutes, I wondered if Dad was going to cave in. Now nothing made my father happier than making a sale, but I learned a valuable lesson that day. He surprised me when he said with humor, "Wayne, I hear you want me to lower the price to $34,000. How 'bout I do this instead? How 'bout $41,000?" Complete silence in the car while an eternity seemingly passed. I thought oh, my dad made a mistake. On the contrary, he knew his customer, his market, and exactly what he was doing! Finally, I heard the man on the other end say with a distinctive Southern accent, "Joe, the $38,000 will be just fine, assuming that price is still available."

I learned then and there, when it comes to learning, there is no substitute for real-life experience. There is no sales class, customer service training, or marketing strategy that would have ever suggested that my father should have replied in the way he did; but as a real business owner, he knew what worked and that business owners "get it" when other business owners speak. Experience in the business world trumps academics. And in a peer council, it is all about sharing real-life experiences.

After my corporate stint, entrepreneurship kept pulling me forward. I was involved in a start- up that raised venture capital, but I found it was a model that didn't suit me—I was reluctant to give control away to shareholders in exchange for what they demanded for the business. My basic core values clashed with the choices of choosing between promoting value to my customers, the employees, or the shareholders. It was always or—never and. So, I did the next most logical thing—I bought a peer advisory franchise.

Helping CEOs, business owners, and entrepreneurs create success is my passion. I went into a

business with resources that should have worked. Unfortunately, after eating a lot of rice and cheese through tough times, I realized that if you build it like the franchise model, I bought taught, you weren't likely to get the results you expected. Increasingly frustrated and not making the money I wanted, I knew I needed something different, something more. Instead of relying solely on the franchise model, I needed to take what I had learned throughout the years and reconfigure the model with a different marketing concept. For me, creating a new model wasn't a choice, but a necessity to survive. Recently I was told that my name, Tina, is an acronym on Wall Street for There Is No Alternative. It was time for me to reinvent, to be innovative, to be... just like my father selling that used concrete mixer, confident. Thus, my strategic partnership model was born.

I figured out a way to build a large, vibrant peer advisory franchise within a small franchise model and make it work, even when the available resources might not be the right ones. And I created the largest, single-owner franchise that sold for the highest value in the entire franchise's history at that time by using many of the concepts I talk about in this book.
I founded LXCouncil, a peer advisory council company, based on my experience of what needs to be different with the

industry: a different way to market and attract the right business owners, CEOs, and entrepreneurs to be in a council and a different way to run the councils. My peer advisory council model caters to and serves business owners who are working hard in their business and who want to work more on their business. It includes those who are ready to strategically rise to another level and who desire to be surrounded by successful peers who can inspire them to get there. Through a peer advisory council model, they can have the richest resources available, resources that utilize the experience and proven business-success strategies of real-life business owners that really work.

How do I know peer advisory councils have that kind of impact? Because I've witnessed it with hundreds of owners. I've watched CEOs grow and gain clarity like never before while they enjoy unprecedented growth in their business and less stress.

I wish I had a dime for every time a CEO told me, "I wish I knew about this concept years ago; if I had only known." If, if, if—don't let that be you! Let me introduce you to your dream team!

PEER ADVISORY COUNCIL ANATOMY

Insight: There is no manual for running a business.

Plans fail for lack of counsel, but with many advisers, they succeed.
- Proverbs 15:22

Peer-to-peer advisory councils are not new—they've been utilized by successful entrepreneurs throughout history. In fact, some sources say they date back to the dawn of civilization, or at least to several thousand years ago when people stopped leading the nomadic existence of hunter-gatherers and began living together in villages and cities instead. Despite the popularity of peer-to-peer councils in certain circles, like at elite levels of the world's top companies, many business owners in the so-called trenches of day-to-day operations don't know what they are or why they're useful. When entrepreneurs find out about the concept, they're often intrigued and want to learn more. So, what exactly is a peer-to-peer council? Let's start with that first.

On one level, the answer is obvious. As I've said, these councils are made of up businesspeople on similar levels of success who have similar responsibilities. That means they all share much in common, even though they're not in the same industry. The participants get together on a regular basis and pool their knowledge to help each other out. On a deeper level, as I indicated, peer advisory councils are an entrepreneur's secret weapon. Members gain access to knowledge and insights that their competitors often lack. That extra edge can really make a big difference in how a company performs in a competitive marketplace.

PEER ADVISORY COUNCILS 101

The peer-to-peer advisory council concept is more than three thousand years old. Yet very few business leaders know what councils are and how they work. A council represents a group of peers put together by a company, such as mine, that facilitates a monthly meeting where CEOs, leaders, and entrepreneurs act as each other's council of advisors. The market is untapped, largely because the concept is little-known and not widely advertised. There's also another reason that's worth mentioning. Business leaders tend to think other leaders can't possibly be having the same challenges. They think they are unique, so the inclination to seek out peers almost seems counterintuitive. I'd have to say the idea doesn't even occur to most CEOs.

By definition, a peer-to-peer council consists of members who have similar levels of experience and authority. Today, peer council members are likely to be business leaders or senior leaders who meet on a regular basis. The key factor is consistency—the same peers meet always at a prescheduled time. The structure of a peer advisory council varies by the organization that is delivering the service. Some groups are self-run, but the most effective ones have a professional moderator to create and manage the council.

It's important to note that both business leaders and their companies can be at different levels and still benefit from a peer advisory group. The important thing to look for is a good pairing of business leaders who are all at the same relative level on a professional basis. The different levels for

CEOs include multiple categories: first-time, new CEOs just learning their roles, CEOs with multiple roles within the company, and seasoned CEOs who have evolved from tactical to strategic roles.

Companies can also be at different levels. You've got start-up companies, established companies branching into new markets, and companies breaking into existing, mature markets. The evolution of each kind of company varies, and so that is something to consider when you look at peer advisory group you might be interested in joining. For a start-up, sales are more important than processes at the beginning. Employees must multitask or fulfill several roles, while other duties are outsourced. At the other extreme is an established company that has enjoyed growth and has multiple layers of management, defined areas of expertise, and a revenue stream and existing clients.

How can these widely varied categories be matched and aligned with the other CEOs in the council? The best way is to define each CEO's specific needs. Do you share the same needs? Is your company a start-up, or is it established? Look at the other members and ask questions. Are the members seeking personal development, or are they most interested in their company's evolution? What experiences have the CEO and the company shared, and where do they want to go? What is the CEO's vision for his or her personal growth and the growth of his or her business? What are the CEO's challenges and opportunities? These kinds of questions and more must be answered to ensure the right fit. Once that information has been processed, CEOs are matched with a group best aligned with their experience and needs. This is the process you'll go through too.

COUNCIL LEVELS

For example, I will illustrate three different levels of councils. For the sake of discussion, I am going to label them entrepreneurial councils, growth councils, and strategic councils.

Entrepreneurial councils: An entrepreneurial council consists of new organizations and new CEOs. They are still developing their internal structure and refining their client offerings. They appear very tactical in day-to-day actions.

Growth councils: In a growth council, CEOs are more experienced and run more established companies; they are focused on expansion within their existing industry or another industry = growth mode. They typically have the company's internal foundation, management structure, and client offerings established. They appear both tactical and strategic in day-to-day actions.

Strategic councils: Strategic councils usually comprise seasoned, mature CEOs who are thinking strategically. They want to expand their market, product, or service and have managers managing managers. It is not uncommon to find both mature lines of business as well as new lines of business within the company.

Each of these three council types requires different processes. Just as suits are tailored to ensure a proper fit, the council must properly match the evolution of the CEO and company. One-size-fits-all is not a standard that a CEO should invoke when seeking a group of peers. To choose a valuable peer council group to join, CEOs must understand their needs and communicate them clearly to the moderator prior to signing up.

Aligning CEOs within a peer council is a strategic process,

which I refer to as the discovery process. The process involves an interview that gathers the information necessary to determine a good fit. It also helps avoid matching a CEO with a peer advisory council that doesn't meet his or her needs or even joining when he or she shouldn't. When that happens, it is an injustice to the new CEO, as well as all of the other council members who are impacted by the decision.

Although it is always good practice to avoid a mistake as much as possible, sometimes a poor fit occurs and creates turnover in the council, which can affect all members negatively. However, let's not forget that some member turnover is unavoidable and can be good for a council. For instance, if a CEO sells a company, transitions to another position, retires, relocates to another area, or has unusual circumstances that require his or her time and attention, the seat left open should be filled with another CEO who will be just as valuable to the council

Peer-to-peer councils are constantly evolving because of several dynamic factors. Either the council is new, and the members are growing together, the council is mature, and the members are advancing from tactical to strategic processes, or the council is an existing one, but the members change from time to time.

YOUR UNBIASED TEAM

Matching members of a council is similar to recruiting. Recruiters strive to match a company with its future employees. But they must also match the future employee with the company. The recruiter must consider the company's needs, the applicant's skills, and the needs and desires of both. Because a good match is crucial, a recruiter doesn't always select from a pool of applicants—sometimes the recruiter does fieldwork to identify and approach a prospective good fit.

Take the same analogy and apply it to the CEO wanting to find the right peer advisory council and the peer advisory council wanting to find the right CEO. Matching peer council members is also likened to building a team. Each member of the team has to be chosen for the contribution he or she can make to the group as a whole. Just as coaches don't choose a player because he or she fits the uniform, members shouldn't choose potential CEOs as peer members just because they will fill an empty chair in their council. A team can only be effective when every member has the experience, background, and ability to contribute to and enhance its overall performance.

A peer-to-peer council must also make sure each and every member strengthens, not weakens, the whole group. In a mature team, such as a college or professional-level team, the process of selecting a new player becomes even more important. The dream team emerges when every member is a valuable participant. It is that type of team that everyone should strive for when considering a peer group or council.

Each CEO needs to feel that it is his or her team. A strategic selection process is essential because otherwise, the odds of each member's success are left to chance. As a peer council member, you need to be involved to make sure it is a right fit for you. You must respect each of your peers, and the group as a whole. After all, you will be receiving feedback from CEOs, and you need to be able to gain and give critical insights. The makeup of your council is critical to its longevity your continued participation in it.

For the council to become your dream team, you must feel integral to its success. CEOs should also consider how much voice they are given when new members join the group. The vetting process is a balance between the members themselves and an experienced peer group organization. If the members are not given a voice in the process, they may want to consider requesting that you and other members be involved, because it's their value at stake.

The moderator should also understand the needs of the CEOs that need to be met. Regardless of those needs, flexibility may be necessary to accommodate members' needs. The process may have to be changed, either occasionally or continually, to align with the needs of the council's members.

These are some of the considerations involved when developing a dream team and strengthening its effectiveness over time. Sports teams change, and so do peer council groups. The moderator is like the sports coach—the person who must understand the team members' abilities and strengths to determine how to make the team its best. As you'll soon see, a top-notch moderator is vital! But even more so is the importance of each member of the council as they come together to share triumphs and failures, and then learn from both.

COUNCIL NUTS AND BOLTS

As previously mentioned, the members of the council must be carefully matched. For councils to be successful, the members must be chosen carefully based on several factors.

Members from noncompeting industries
To prevent conflicts of interest from clouding the advice given by council members, there can only be one member from each specific industry, that is, only one electrical, insurance, marketing, commercial construction company, or any other industry.

Objectivity and transparency
All relationships must be disclosed and scrutinized before members are admitted to a council. A peer cannot sit on a council with a business owner who employs one of his or her

close friends or family members. Council discussions are highly confidential. Members can be tempted to disclose sensitive information to their friends or family members. The existence of an affiliated relationship could cause a member to give biased feedback. All relationships between peers must be at arm's length or greater. There cannot be even a remote possibility of conflict, and the following scenario describes why.

News from the Trenches

While establishing a council in a resort community I frequented all my summers as a kid—a small town of less than 80,000—I realized that many of the business leaders knew or had been closely acquainted with each other. The connections themselves weren't the surprise—it was the depth of those connections. Most leaders had conducted business with the other leaders or had family members or friends who worked for them. Because of the interconnections, many relationships had become strained, and some business leaders had preconceived opinions of how the other leaders ran their businesses. Everyone had a label: ethical, professional, hardworking, lazy, and so on; you get the picture.

I was considering adding to the council a particular marketing company, which happened to have an existing council member as a client. It was a temporary project, so it was unlikely that a conflict would emerge. I was also considering an insurance company but discovered that the owner's wife worked for the marketing company—a scenario that would violate confidentiality. The marketing company owner could not openly discuss his company plans if they would negatively affect his employees, one of whom was a council member's wife. The myriad conflicts of interest forced me to choose a different insurance company owner to sit on that council.

No member conflicts

Conflicts can present themselves in many different ways. When choosing council members, not only do we ensure that competing industries don't sit on the same council, but we also ensure that the council contains no member's clients, vendors, suppliers, or investors. Strict adherence to this rule maintains the council's integrity. Another rule is that business partners cannot participate on the same council. It is unconditional that the atmosphere is open and candid, with no possibility that anyone has a potential vested interest in a member's business. For that reason, only one owner from each company can participate in a particular council. Partners cannot participate on a joint basis. This prevents potential arguments, discussions, and debates between two members that might require other council members to act as mediators or referees. Multiple leaders or partners can sit on different councils.

Council Size
Council sizes can vary greatly. The average number of members ranges from eight to twelve per group. As a member, you need a group large enough to provide diverse experiences and opinions, yet small enough for intimate conversations. You need vulnerability to develop, while having enough time to ask for feedback on your struggles or questions you want others' insights on. Also, you want a large enough group that absent members don't affect discussions nor reduce the group's energy or dynamic. It is a personal decision of the group and the moderator to have the right number and mix of members that provide the ultimate value. Choose an organization that takes council membership seriously and doesn't just add members to boost its own revenue.

Meeting frequency
Most meetings are held monthly, usually at the same time and on the same day. Consistency allows members to schedule their commitments around the meetings, thus increasing the likelihood of full attendance. If not mandatory, attendance should be expected as a high priority. It is disrespectful when a member does not attend regularly. The other members count on each other to be present and offer their opinions,

insights, and experience. When members are absent, they are missed, and they disappoint their peers.

As an owner, you can expect to spend up to four hours or more a month with your peers working to improve your business. Meetings are either one half-day or one full day once each month. Depending on the organization you choose, the four-hour meetings may have eight to twelve members involved, and the full-day meetings may have up to twelve to sixteen or more members.

If you think that's a lot of time to spend each month just talking to your peers, please think again! As one bank president recently asked me when trying to understand the benefits of a peer-to-peer council, "How can any business owner spend half a day away from their business?" That question concerned me, especially because it came from a bank president who dealt closely with many business leaders in the community. The best response to his questions came from one of my members, who stated, "How can any business owner not take time out to work on their business? In fact, if they don't, they are being irresponsible to the future of their company."

> *"If you are not taking time to work on your business, you are not being responsible as the owner."*
> *— Paul, National Distribution Company, MO*

At the request of their members, some councils skip meetings during summer months and holidays. Some councils skip a month's meeting and replace it with a double meeting or a retreat. The key is to meet regularly and not go for long periods between meetings. Otherwise, momentum slows, the sense of connection wanes, and the sense of urgency declines. The council should be able to have input as to what works for them as a group. As the group matures, the meeting frequency may change to match the evolving needs of its members.

News from the Trenches

Ann walked into her office after a long weekend to find a Post-it note on her desk. The note announced the resignation of her partner, who wanted out immediately. Based on their partnership agreement, Ann owed her partner a large sum of money very soon. Besides the financial challenge of the payoff, Ann also faced the loss of a key leader, who ran essential aspects of her business.

She was so panicked that she called her peer advisory council moderator, who suggested a special meeting just for her. Her peer council gladly met to help Ann decide which actions to take and when. This impromptu, productive meeting demonstrates the benefit of being involved in a peer-to-peer council: when you need help—big help—it is there. I've found many members of the groups I've worked with over the years cite the close connections among the participants as playing a vital factor in the ongoing success of their businesses.

Meeting structure

The meeting structure can vary depending on the organization. For example, all council members discuss their challenges, opportunities, problems, or ideas. This is something I abbreviate as the group's COPIs. The key is to find a meeting style that has structure but is flexible to members' needs. All councils should have their own nuances that fit its members' culture. They all follow the same foundation of what makes the meetings high-impact but have the flexibility of what works for them. As an example, one of our company's councils opens its meeting with "Steve's Useless Trivia." Before a meeting started, one of the members began reciting random facts. Now his peers expect it, so it's on every month's agenda. It's funny, it helps the members bond with one another, and it starts the meeting on a positive tone. As a bonus, no members are ever late— they don't want to miss the opening dialogue!

Meeting focus

As a business owner or leader, your time is valuable. Chatting about random topics will not be a productive way to gain insights to help improve your business or spend your time. Many organizations have no structure, and after a while, leaders get frustrated by their lack of direction, purpose, and focus. A lack of focus can cause many peer members to leave a group. When considering a group, ask about meeting structure.

Some councils invite speakers, some go on retreats, some do strategic plans, some involve member presentations, some plan social events, some have educational content, and some don't do any of these. The core mission remains the same, though. The group works together to help each other, and their businesses become more successful, as well as to help the members be happier in their jobs.

You should also inquire about guidelines. How consistent is attendance? Are the members committed? Do the meetings start and end on time? Remember, your time is valuable; if a council can't respect start times and end times, disrespect can become pervasive. Members may assume they can arrive ten or twenty minutes late and not miss anything. Eventually, some members will feel fine missing the whole meeting. Lack of accountability is the moderator's fault. Be sure to screen for this when determining a right-fit group for you.

Financial commitment

Many factors determine the price you might pay to sit on a peer-to-peer council. The more formal the meeting, the greater the financial commitment. The cost will also depend upon your geographical area, the size and sophistication of your business, your experience as a CEO, and the involvement of your moderator.

At one end of the spectrum, a member might pay nothing to

PEER ADVISORY COUNCIL ANATOMY

participate in an informal meeting that functions without a moderator. On the other end of the spectrum, a member may pay thousands of dollars a year for a formal meeting with an experienced, articulate moderator. Some organizations require monthly payment, while others require quarterly or annual payments.

YOU SHOULD KNOW...

A peer advisory council is not a place to meet with your friends or to make new ones. It's also not a place to identify prospective clients or business partners. It's not even a networking group—although some loosely refer to it as such. Networking would have the potential to create conflict, as stated earlier. The meetings are not social events; they are structured, focused meetings that achieve a stated purpose: to help each other address business ideas, problems, and growth in a trusting and open environment through their own experiences, insights, and perspectives.

The members of a peer-to-peer council should not be considered fiduciaries. Fiduciary responsibilities or liabilities are reserved for a formal board of directors or officers, where there is an expectation of disclosure. Because they must adhere to the highest standard of confidentiality, peer advisory councils do not have that expectation.

Peer advisory councils are not new, but business leaders often confuse them with other groups, such as advisory boards. The concepts of peer advisory councils and advisory boards may sound similar, but they are, in fact, quite different.

A peer advisory council consists of a group of peers you rely on for unbiased advice, insight, perspective, opinion, comment, expertise, experience, and accountability. It is also your own group of advisors who look through the windshield versus the rearview mirror. Their purpose is to see and strive for what lies ahead, not what's behind.

A rearview mirror is much smaller than a windshield, and for good reason. Its purpose is to provide a short and limited view that can be considered when moving forward. The rearview mirror only reflects the limited scope of what is behind you and the past. The windshield shows a much bigger picture— your vision. Remember, you can go only forward, which is where opportunity exists.

Advisory boards and peer advisory councils have different purposes depending on your expectations or where you are in your business.

ON PEER ADVISORY BOARDS

An advisory board might be formed to serve as a formal advice group for a start-up. It could comprise professional advisors, such as an accountant, an attorney, an insurance broker, your banker, a family member, or an investor. Initially, a young company might use an advisory board that meets monthly, quarterly, or annually. One difference between this type of advisory board and a peer advisory council is that advisory board members will have a financial interest in your business. They usually are compensated for their participation, sometimes with equity in the business or with nice dinners, travel, and expenses paid. Because peer advisory council members do not have a vested interest in your company, their advice will be unbiased. Council members are not paid to give advice, but rather they pay the organization leading the council meetings.

Advisory board members can give thoughtful advice. But that advice does not always come from a business-oriented perspective. It often comes from a professional perspective, which is vastly different from a peer advisory council. In addition, because they are professionals who are hired to

26

provide services for your business, advisory board members often charge you for their time and their advice.

At the initial stages, advisory board members might be a business owner's friends and family members. Those are the people whom the owner trusts and can afford. Most often, family members or friends sit on advisory boards for free. And we all know how useful free advice is!

Because of their biased advice, advisory boards can sometimes be the worst kind of boards. Business leaders have to be cautious with the intent of the advice they are given. Are advisory board members being open, or are they hiding what needs to be said? Are they afraid of hurting your feelings? As a business owner, will you be open to their comments, be defensive, or dismiss them?

Biases naturally exist between family members or friends because the personal relationship plays a key role. If you decide to choose an advisory board, remember this: the relationship between such members and the business owner will affect the value and effectiveness of their advice. Personal relationships can easily be damaged because of advisory boards. Mixing family and business comes with risks requiring careful consideration.

At some point, a business owner might need his or her own board of advisors to provide input that he or she cannot get either inside the business or from other professionals. The difference between having a shared peer-to-peer council and having your own group of advisors is that your own group has a strategic and specific purpose. Each member is handpicked for what he or she brings to the table. For instance, successful professionals might provide a useful skill or access to a desired market. That professional supplements your existing team, filling in any skill gaps and providing a higher level of expertise that you cannot afford.

News from the Trenches

Let's take a brief look at a guy named Larry. To help him expand into new fiber-optic network markets, Larry developed this type of advisory board to supplement his peer council membership. Larry sought professionals who would be invested in his success and would bring insights and experience into his desired market, the medical field in particular.

To fill his team's skill gaps, Larry found specialists to sit on his advisory board, such as a medical doctor and government medical specialists. He held quarterly meetings with an agenda and expectations. It was these advisors who helped him develop his industry-specific strategic plan. With his new contacts and resources, he shortened his time to market.

Larry's advisory board is the most expensive. Generally, a business owner must pay the advisory board members, either in money or equity, for their participation. You can expect to compensate these members for their time, whether it's paying a stipend, buying them dinner, or paying for their travel. Because their time is limited and valuable, members require a carefully crafted agenda and much planning on the business owner's part.

ADVISORY COUNCIL TYPES

Peer-to-peer councils, in which members serve as advisors to each other, have different levels of participation and commitment. These councils can be offered and managed by associations, industry groups, individuals, or companies specializing in putting peer councils together.

MASTERMIND GROUPS

Mastermind groups are an example of a simple peer-to-peer group. This type of group is informal, consisting of casual discussions moderated by the members themselves. One such group was the Vagabonds. Its members comprised Henry Ford, Thomas Edison, President Warren G. Harding, and Harvey Firestone—all business leaders from different industries who worked together to provide each other with advice and accountability. This group of prestigious individuals proves not only that peer groups are an established concept, but also that peer groups are effective for businesspeople at all levels, even the most successful and renowned.

PEER COUNCILS

On a higher level are the companies that assemble peer councils full- time. These companies hire an unbiased moderator to facilitate the meetings and provide structure, process, and experience, while ensuring that each member benefits from his or her participation. The company also facilitates the recruitment of new members to create an unbiased peer-to-peer group.

The potential benefits should dictate which type of group a business owner pursues. My definition of ROI is not return on investment; it's return on involvement. On a spectrum of determining the right type of group is the level of return on involvement that you will require and need.

> **ROI: Return on Involvement**
>
> What every business owner needs to look for when evaluating a peer group

The majority of small business leaders prefer peer-to-peer councils because they require less planning, time, and expense. The business owner doesn't just receive advice— he or she serves others with his or her expertise and advice, too. Fees are the cost business leaders pay to benefit from their involvement in the council.

SPECIALTY COUNCILS

What are specialty councils? They serve an industry niche. Associations may have a council as an added value to their members who are in the same industry. That association will cater to a particular cause or industry. Consider the National Electrical Contractors Association or the National Automobile Dealers Association 20 Group, for example. Within these groups, there will be a mutual interest among the members and an opportunity for members to learn best practices in their industry. Specialty councils commonly meet quarterly at a member's location or at the association's conference. They share financials and discuss specific key benchmarks to rank their performance against a competitor's in a different location.

One caution in specialty groups is groupthink. It's easy for specialty councils to address challenges the same way they always have. Some challenges require outside perspectives and ideas. Often, people from the same industry have the same opinions and mind-set, and they cannot see beyond the scope of their experience. In addition, because these groups can meet only quarterly or annually, during specific events such as conferences and so on, the members may change on a frequent basis. It may be difficult to forge relationships within the council or to hold members accountable for their initiatives.

Within the specialty classification is another type of council, industry-related but not industry-specific. Successful industry-specific councils can be in manufacturing, construction, information technology, or professional services. They differ from associations that serve a particular industry classification. In industry-related councils, members don't compete for the same customer. In the construction industry, there might be electrical, mechanical, engineering, roofing, insulation, paving, architecture, and so on, companies represented. The manufacturing industry is also broad, covering the manufacturing of many different types of products that serve many different industries. Though members' products and customers may differ, their challenges will be common. They speak the same industry language, share related resources, and have a deeper understanding of the nuances of each other's businesses. A specialty peer council can be an asset to businesses by allowing them to benefit from each other's experience and specialization.

When it comes to business issues, it is understood that 80 percent of them are shared and 20 percent of them are unique. Niche specialty councils help close the 20 percent gap. Let's use a construction specialty council as an example of the power that such a council can provide. At one such meeting, a member brought up an issue with a surety bond on a particular job with a general contractor. The GC was changing the requirements, putting the leadership on the shoulders of the subcontractor, an electrician. The electrician asked his council for the best way to word the language to protect his company and how to address the issue with their bond insurance company to mitigate the level of obligation they were limited to receive. Because everyone was knowledgeable of construction, there was no need to define terms such as "surety bond." After some discussion, the members clarified the issue, which was whether the general contractor could make that demand on the electrical subcontractor. It was a conversation that required peers who understood the intricacies of the situation: what bonds meant to the industry and their potential impact on the electrician. The subcontractor later approached the general contractor, who realized that it was inappropriate to pass his liability on to an electrician. The subcontractor had experienced an enlightening, invaluable discussion that he could not have gotten in another type of council.

Another specialty-council type serves those in a certain profession, such as chief financial officers, operations managers, project managers, human resource directors, or sales executives. They all work for different companies and are rarely the owner of a business. The council's purpose is to address challenges specific to their positions in the company.

For example, a council of sales executives might focus only on sales-related topics, such as compensation plans, the sales structure, selling techniques, territorial challenges, quotas, and customer issues. Make note: these councils are not owner councils, but key executive councils. They also help key executive members develop contacts outside of the company. Many key executives only have the owner, not a network of peers, to bounce ideas off. Sometimes that is less than ideal. Being involved with peers helps with their own personal development and provides time to work on their own areas of the business proactively and innovatively.

Specialty councils can also include other types, including faith-based, female-owned businesses, or young business leaders. These councils are appealing to leaders who want advice from members who share their values, beliefs, or challenges.

Because of their uniqueness, specialty councils can be difficult to locate. It requires effort to find and assemble such a group, and the market must be large enough to support such a council.

As you can see, there are many types of advisory boards and peer councils, each of which serves a different purpose, has different members, and provides benefits depending on the stage of business growth. In spite of established characteristics, each council meeting may vary in terms of frequency, participation, format, and the investment a business owner or member would be required to make.

INSIGHTS

- Peer advisory councils: a three-thousand-year-old concept.
- There are over 3,500 councils that meet monthly in the United States. They are proven to help leaders with their journey to success.
- Not all councils are created equal. Structure is important such as
  - frequency of the meetings
  - investment to participate
  - size of the group
  - unbiased, noncompeting members
  - no conflict of interest between members or the moderator
  - meeting format
  - fiduciary responsibility or not
- Specialty councils are unique.
- They serve a specific purpose that aligns with members' values.
- The stage of your business, the level of growth, and the amount of change desired will influence the type of council or board that fits your specific needs.

HOMEWORK ANYONE?

Yes, I know. The last thing you want is more work to do. After all, you're a busy and successful business leader. But every now and then in this book, I am going to ask you to stop, think, and cash in. You'll need to do this before

> Is your company remarkable so that others remark about it?

you can sit down, speak up, and cash in as a participant in a vibrant and inspiring peer advisory **group**. Your self-improvement and enhanced business success starts at home, as it were, so it's important for you to get at least a little bit introspective at this point. If this is hard for you, rest assured that you're not alone. Some of the most highly successful people I've ever met don't like to really be alone with their thoughts. It's important for your mind-set ranking, though. You have to make the time to actually do almost nothing at least for a little while every week, and preferably every day. Downtime is vital to the growth of your business. Downtime is important for you on many levels, both professionally and personally.

You've all heard about the power of positive thinking. Norman Vincent Peale made that whole concept famous in the first half of the twentieth century, and charismatic leaders in politics, religion, and business have been spouting off about the power of positive thinking ever since. I'm a firm believer in positive thinking, but that alone won't change much. You've got to do more than just think positively to get ahead in today's business environment.

Ask yourself this question: "Have I reached my full potential?"

If you're like most CEOs, you're probably not even close. In fact, when we ask our CEOs this question, they consistently answer that they are only at around 20 percent of their potential. There is no right answer; it's personal to you. But if you are a CEO, you have great potential. Are you using it? Of course, you are, but how much of your potential are you really tapping into?

What if you could increase your potential by just 5 percent? How would that affect your company? What positive impact would that have on your results? Can you quantify it?

How would that affect your mind-set? When you grow personally, your company and your team grow, too. You enhance the growth process when you surround yourself with your peers at growing organizations.

Why do companies fail to reach their potential? In short, it's mainly because of their CEOs.

As the CEO, you are solely responsible for the growth of your company. To put it bluntly, you must grow if

> *"Any good leader wants to hear multiple viewpoints."*
> - Wes, Architectural Design Firm, VA

your company is to grow. The two-go hand in hand. If the CEO is at his or her capacity, the company is too. The CEO must continue to grow personally and professionally so the organization can prosper. To do that, CEOs must spend time doing what they do best: driving value to the company, what only they can do as the CEO, and what adds the most value because when they do it, it makes big impacts. These are the activities that create big results.

When you participate in a peer advisory council, consider it a stepping-stone to enhance your personal growth and realize your greatest potential. You will be pushed out of your comfort zone to new frontiers. Being slightly uncomfortable enables growth.

Take a moment to rank your mind-set in relation to owning your business. Write it down, even if just in the margins of this book. Writing it down will give you greater reflection and a foundation to come back later and see if your mind-set is higher or lower and why. Writing down your answers to these questions is no different than writing down your goals or your vision. The most successful among us are able to visualize their goals. Most can only do that if they write those goals down, refine the goals, and add to those goals as the person and the goals evolve together. When written down, your goals become real.

So, get out a pen and paper. Don't use your computer unless you must. The physical act of writing is key here, which is why I'm steering you away from your keyboard.

Assignment

How do you rank your mind-set? _____
Rank from a scale of 1 (lowest) to 10 (highest).

If your mind-set is not a 10, how can you make it a 10? What needs to happen for your mind-set to improve?

If your mind-set is a 10, what makes it so high? Why do you have no room for improvement? What can you do to sustain a 10?

Business accelerator action: Name one action you can take today that will help your mind-set stay consistently higher. Record it and refer to it until accomplished.

2

WHY JOIN A PEER ADVISORY COUNCIL?

Insight: Epiphanies can be intentional, not serendipitous

*Lonely at the top? You don't have to be! - Roger Goodell,
Commissioner, National Football League*

I have yet to find a comprehensive how-to manual for running a company. I believe that is because there is no exact science in doing so; running a business is not cookie-cutter. If it were, more people would do it and we'd all be successful. But no two situations are exactly the same. There are nuances that are all different at any point in time, like the competition, your team, and the economy, to name a few. With those differences, solutions are not the same.

It can be very lonely operating as an owner or CEO, particularly if you do not have a partner or partners and when there is no manual. Who do you talk to? Who can you confide in? Who can check your thinking? Who can inspire you with new ideas?

The short answer is your peers can help you help yourself and your company while you simultaneously do the same thing for them. That's simply the beauty of joining a peer advisory group. As I said earlier, the benefits work on both a surface and a deep level. The benefits are the sole reason you'd participate.

I've been including snippets from the so-called trenches of business to assist in making my points. Let's go into some depth now, where you'll find several detailed illustrations to think about. First, meet Bill! He's having a very bad day!

News from the Trenches

It's shortly after seven o'clock in the morning, and as usual, Bill is already putting out fires. While driving his company truck to his first peer council meeting, he's on a conference call with his management team. Bill needs a solution to his latest problem: how to please the general contractor without cutting into his construction company's profits. Why does Bill always have to be the one to have all the solutions, all the right answers? Why can't his senior project manager, Todd, fix this? Todd has been with him for a long time and should know how to do this.

He wonders why Todd hasn't taken care of this issue and, instead, let it get this far. As a business owner, have you ever felt like Bill? When there is a mistake in your company, who owns it? Who makes it right? Who ensures it doesn't happen again? And who pays the price? As in Bill's situation, he will bear the consequences because he is the owner. It's always the owner's money, reputation, and expense at stake. As CEO, Bill has experienced this scenario far too many times. Bill's problem was this: his largest client, a general contractor, wanted to change the design from the initial blueprint that Bill based his bid on. The underlying problem wasn't just the change—in this case, it's the way the situation is being handled by Todd. This wasn't the first time Bill had to intervene to solve a client issue after Todd had mismanaged it. Todd has shown a consistent lack of communication and an inability to anticipate problems.

Bill knew the client was wrong, but Todd's mismanagement had put his company on the defensive. With little time to spare, Bill had to keep his client on good terms while preventing further damage and profit loss. With the phone still in his hand, Bill sighed and shook his head, wondering why he was continually plagued with these situations.

As Bill neared the building to attend the council meeting, he wound his conference call to an end. His first thought was that he didn't have time to attend the meeting. He was already working fifty-five to sixty-five hours a week, and today, like most days, his business and employees needed him. Bill shook his head and sighed, wondering how other CEOs did it. He must not have the secret. There never seemed to be enough time in the day. No matter how much time he spent working, he never seemed to approach the vision he once had for his business. Still, he had nothing to lose by attending his first peer council meeting. He parked the truck and went inside.

Slipping his phone into his pocket, Bill entered and first saw the My Transition™ chart. He was being asked to rank his mind-set at that moment on a scale of 1 to 10, with 1 being the lowest and 10 being the highest. It was only 8:00 a.m., and Bill ranked his mind-set as a 2.

At times like these, Bill felt exhausted, knowing that he carried the burden of creating solutions. That certainly wasn't what he envisioned when he started his business. Every day, another unknown or obstacle seemed to appear. Bill wished he had someone he could count on to provide him with advice and a different perspective. He wanted to make the right decisions, but he knew he didn't have all the answers. Plus, he had nobody to share his concerns that understood. He couldn't share his company setbacks with his wife, nor could he confide in his employees or his competitors. Bill needed unbiased feedback, but he'd quickly learned that business leaders like him lack a supportive network. It was, indeed, lonely at the top.

Does Bill's morning sound familiar? Do you hit the ground running before you even get your foot out the door in the morning? Are your workdays twelve to fourteen hours long on weekdays and/or on weekends? Long hours are a common complaint among business leaders, who often need downtime more than anything. At the meeting, Bill had several problems he needed to solve—not only to enjoy the benefits of owning his own company, but also to keep his business growing. Bill already knows how to run a successful business, but he knows it can be even better, more successful.

When I met Bill, he was frustrated and tired of being tired. Bill had confidence from owning a multimillion-dollar business, but he wanted it to be so much better. I could see Bill was confident on the outside. Unfortunately, every decision Bill made was the result of trial and error. Bill has a good business that provides a quality service. But he knows that there is no handbook that tells business leaders how to overcome the daily challenges they're certain to face. The security and flexibility he thought would come with being his own boss were nowhere in sight. Unfortunately, Bill's predicament is all too common among business leaders.

As Bill began attending the council meetings, I noticed a change come over him that I'd seen before. He and his peers shared the angst of owning or running a busy company with each other, and the discourse offered on how to best manage the negativity, the operations snags, the ineptitude of others that occasionally created problems, the joys and triumphs of successful ventures, the freedom entrepreneurship can bring, and so much more contributed toward an ability for everyone in the group to form close bonds. In Bill's case, he felt much less isolated and less isolated and adrift in indecision.

Bill's Benefits

As you review the benefits Bill received after joining a peer advisory council, consider whether those same benefits would be of value to you. I suspect you will think so!

- Enhanced leadership ability: Bill learned over subsequent peer meetings that his project manager was not the right fit in that role. He received the insight from his peer council to realize that he needed to make a change with Todd.

- Bolstered self-confidence: Bill discovered new techniques, technology, and innovation from others that he applied to his own business. He became more educated in all aspects of business, and he realized he didn't have to have all the answers.
- Increased accountability: By talking about his goals, strategy to get there, and vision, Bill became far more focused. His energy increased. He spent less time at work worrying about micromanaging. The main reason this occurred stemmed from the fact that his peer group held him accountable for the progress of his own personal and business growth.
- Disciplined big-picture thinking: Bill could now spend his time on the 20 percent of the opportunities that would drive 80 percent of the future of the company. Leaders like Bill want to spend time on these activities and get frustrated when they don't. They gain energy when they can and lose energy when they are in the weeds. The best use

> "This provides me with a structured discipline to stage and reach my goals. The camaraderie of my fellow board members, although concentrated in a four-hour period, is caring, genuine, honest, and loyal. My investment has already provided me the best business return in 20 years"
> -Cynthia,
> Bed & Breakfast, MD

of leaders', CEOs', or entrepreneurs' talent is on what they do best—and if they are not doing it, who is watching out for the company's future and creating the next big opportunity?
- Decreased operational expenses: Bill began to save money through efficiencies, better decisions, and resource sharing.
- Increased profitability: By gaining feedback from his peers, Bill identified new opportunities to grow the business he might otherwise not have considered.
- Improved recruitment: Bill found the right employee, who

became his general manager. He was reminded how critical it is to have top talent in the key roles in the company.

- Effective delegation strategies: Bill could now delegate and concentrate on the strategy of the company, less on the day-to-day tactical aspects.

- Higher mind-set ranking: Remember how Bill ranked his mind-set at a 2 in his first meeting, and it wasn't even 8:00 a.m.? Bill is not alone: The majority of new peer council members also rank their mind-sets low, even if they run successful businesses. After new members begin to experience the benefits of their peer council, however, they rank their mind-sets consistently higher, regardless of what is happening in their businesses. The peer-to-peer council gives them support, experiences, insights, and confidence. As a result, new members become healthier, less stressed, and more effective in their businesses.

Birds of a Feather

We've now taken a good look at how Bill benefited from joining a peer advisory group. It should be clear why those who participate choose to do so, but let me point out another thing. When you are a member of a group of like-minded individuals in the business world, you are sharing an obvious common characteristic that's worth mentioning in spite of the fact it might sound dumb at first. Here goes! You own businesses!

Yes, that's right! Sometimes thinking about the most obvious thing in the world can be very informative if you look below the surface. Your business is usually your biggest asset, which means you need to protect it. Your peers feel the same way. You want very much to have a successful company. You care about the employees, you want to leave a legacy, and you want to make a difference. You share still another thing in common with your peers. You're not a worker bee. In fact, some might even say you're unemployable, which makes taking steps to ensure that the business thrives very important. You probably don't have any choice if your business goes bust, at least in terms of finding a regular job. You might scoff and say you're highly employable if the whole deal goes south. But if you really get down to brass tacks, you may have to admit that some of your best employees are probably better suited to go out in the job market than you are.

Why are business leaders often perceived as unemployable rather than prized assets for hire? The reason is that business leaders become accustomed to answering to themselves. They can't imagine working for anyone else again. Nor could they. Business leaders make the decisions, create the vision, and drive the company culture. They operate like the slogan on President Harry S. Truman's desk: "The buck stops here." They are the head honchos, the ones who decide the direction of the company, the ones who make the strategic decisions. They are the go-to guys.

Business leaders are independent: they want, need, and expect control. An employee does not get that privilege. It's why original leaders are often jettisoned after a merger or acquisition. Business leaders become outcasts because they can't transition to an employee mentality or minority-owner status. It is hard for them to become the incredible resource that was intended.

The success or failure of the business falls entirely on your shoulders. It's unreasonable to assume you can get a job if your business fails. First, a failure is not a good selling point on your resume. Second, it's almost impossible to happily go from being an employer to an employee.

There is no better alternative

Where else can you hold the jersey for others to wear? Where else do you have an opportunity to really build something far more meaningful than working for someone else? The reward is so much more. Reward can come in the form of financial reward, contribution to society, providing a good living standard for your team, and many other forms. It's an amazing opportunity.

A peer advisory council increases your odds for success. It helps you protect one of, if not the, biggest asset, your company. It helps you be the best head honcho you can be.

As we can see, Bill derived some very tangible business benefits that justified why he would join a peer advisory group. Let's take a close look at a couple more case histories to further

> You hold the jersey for others to wear.

illustrate why you might want to share your knowledge and experiences with peers in a noncompeting team environment without the stress of fiduciary or monetary responsibilities. With a peer advisory council, it's your teammates who really count. On the reciprocating end, it's you and your company that matter too. You not only want to protect your business because in all likelihood it's all you have, but you also want to grow the business to ensure its future, your future, and the futures of everyone who works for you.

Growth is more than an increase in bottom-line profits or top-line revenues. It also involves the personal and professional growth of a company's CEO or owner. One of the main reasons leaders join a peer-to-peer council is that they realize they are stuck. They are stuck with the same thinking. They are stuck with the same problems and same solutions. They are stuck with the same results. They aren't growing, for whatever reason. Some CEOs admit they don't have the answers, but others blame the economy, their marketing plan, or a lack of talent. It's difficult to put things in the right perspective when there are so many factors.

Joining a peer advisory council will give you the ability to avail yourself of a new way of thinking about your business. You free yourself from the status quo of doing things the way the industry does them or the way you have always done them. A mistake leader make is thinking their way is the only way. It's hard to give up and delegate when you believe no one else could possibly do it better. Guess what? If you've got a first-rate management team, you've got people who can and should do it better so that you can concentrate on the top 20 percent of the business that will generate 80 percent of the profits. It's all about the big-picture. It's called the 80/20 principle, and it's something you should practice every day you're at the office.

Now let's meet Melissa!

News from the Trenches
Melissa runs a publishing company that produces a high-end community magazine every month. Melissa had just a few pages available for ads, yet she was constantly asked to donate additional ad space for local charities. Month after month, she struggled to generate ad revenue because of the additional expense of adding more pages. She had no idea how she could increase profits while maintaining the quality of her magazine and also not offending anyone in the community. How does she balance both demands?

When Melissa attended her first council meeting, she was out of ideas. She assumed that every option would upset her customers and key influencers in the community, leaving her to always struggle with the bottom line. But there were other options. Melissa just couldn't see them. Luckily, her council members thought of solutions based on their own experiences. They showed her that there is always an option to pursue in favor of the status quo. Melissa put a policy in place for nonrevenue-generating ads. She communicated to the community that it was now on a first come first serve basis, with a certain amount of availability. She shifted the burden of accepting all requests from her shoulders to the shoulders of the charities. Melissa created a budget for nonrevenue advertising so she made sure to manage the requests accordingly. This kept her in line with her revenue goals and profits. She was able to spend less time on random requests by accepting them a few times a year. She reduced the feeling of guilt because no longer was it perceived as a personal decision by Melissa in the community but as a business decision.

Melissa benefited from her peer advisory group much in the same way Bill did. The solutions Melissa gained from her peers helped her increase profits while maintaining positive business relationships. Thanks to her council, Melissa is now unstuck. She can begin to grow to the next level.

Growth can mean different things to different people. One owner's goal might be to create single- digit sales growth, or it might be to enter a new market or to improve operational efficiencies. Another owner may seek professional growth as a CEO. Different factors weigh into establishing goals, but the fact remains that there must be growth in order for a company to survive, much less thrive. The degree and type of growth is up to the owner's vision and overall strategic plan. Regardless of the type and amount of growth you're seeking, joining a peer-to-peer council is one way to guarantee that you will enjoy personal and business growth. Both are essential. Both together can mean the difference between a lackluster career path as a CEO and one that charts the path of your company all the way to the far-distant stars!

While we're on a roll here, let's take another quick look at an entrepreneur like you. His name is Mark, and he lives to micromanage everything, even though he knows that's a really bad idea. How often do you feel like doing that? Micromanaging, I mean. I know as business leaders, whether you own your company, or you run one for others, you probably feel like you can do most every high-level job yourself. You only delegate because you must, and I bet you don't like it most of the time. You know about the 80/20 principle, the notion that says 80 percent of the profits come from the top 20 percent of the combined effort of your team.

The 80/20 principle is definitely something you should think about. You know in your heart that

> *"One of the greatest values received is having 10 people with different levels of expertise, different scopes of businesses - completely different than mine - learning how they apply their thought processes to problems. [It] is invaluable to me."*
>
> *- Joanne, Jewelry Claim Services, MO*

80 percent of the effort in your organization is spent on maintaining the status quo. And yet you do nothing more than behave as a glorified manager instead of focusing on that top 20 percent of business that will generate 80 percent of your profits. If I am describing you, and I suspect that may well be the case, don't feel too badly about it. We're mostly all in the same boat. I know Mark was when I met him while I was managing a peer advisory council program, he participated in.

News from the Trenches
Mark has owned a commercial refrigeration company for years. As a manager and owner, he is very hands- on, involved in every aspect of the business. Nothing happens without Mark's knowledge and input. When his company added staff, Mark sat through the interviews and made the final hiring decisions. Not only did he scout and hire every technician and driver, but it also wasn't uncommon for Mark to hop in the truck and accompany them on service calls. It was no secret that Mark knew everything that went on in his business every day.

Mark had a highly competent chief financial officer who watched the company's numbers very closely. But Mark hadn't given his CFO any authority. Mark's sales staff knew that if they needed a bid or special pricing, they had to contact Mark. Every decision crossed his desk.

As a business owner, Mark had a vision. He wanted his company to be nationwide, not just regional. He wanted to secure national contracts and service restaurant chains and other institutions. He'd already taken steps toward that growth: his product was manufactured in China, and he private-labeled his own line of refrigeration. But even though Mark had been proactive, his business seemed stuck. Mark couldn't get it to the next level like he envisioned. Why? Not having the trust or talent in the company to delegate is a very common mistake among many leaders.

When Mark joined a peer advisory council, he admitted that his company had a weakness: sales. It was something that he'd struggled with since the beginning. He thought he didn't have time to improve the sales division—like so many business leaders, he was too busy working in his business. That meant riding with a driver or hiring the next technician. Mark's peer advisory council helped him see that any growth in the business would require him to step back and rely on his employees' talent and skills. Mark had to get out of the way. He needed to do what he did best while trusting his employees to do what they did best.

Mark listened to the experiences of his peer-to-peer council, and he began putting their insights into practice. He stopped being so involved in the daily operations, eventually allowing his CFO to make financial decisions and technicians' manager to handle hiring. Mark was then able to make real strides toward his vision of real market growth.

Mark's Benefits

Remember Bill? Well, let's take a quick look at some additional peer advisory benefits from Mark's perspective.

- **Ideas:** Mark set up an in-house sales process and documented it. This allowed him to trust that those in sales would be focused on the right activities. He did the same for hiring truck drivers.
- **Talent:** Mark let go of a nonperforming salesperson, creating a new benchmark for the right talent with the help of his council. He hired a sales manager who had expertise and let him build the team.
- **Accountability:** Mark's peer council held him accountable for letting go. He discovered how to manage to get results without having to actually do the work.
- **Doing what you do best:** Mark is now a better leader, his team is happier, and more is getting done faster. That is because he is concentrating on the activities an owner should be focused on and managing the activities to get there—not doing them himself.

You may not own a third-generation family business that needs to reinvent itself or find new leadership. But like Mark, I bet your business is not the same today as it was a few years ago. If there is one constant in life, besides death and taxes, it's change. Change will come even if you don't want it to. You can't stop it. It's like the tide. It's as constant as the stars, and yet even the stars aren't inert. They're not even as constant as the tide, which changes day to day as well. Stars blaze brightly for an unimaginably long time, and then they morph into supernovas. Black holes in space, what a concept! Do you want your business to be a star? Of course! But you don't want it (or you) to be a black hole that sucks all matter into its apparently infinite void of antimatter. On the contrary, you wouldn't be a business owner or leader unless your star depended on growing your company and enhancing the self-empowerment and prosperity of your employees. Change is your friend. Embrace it!

INSIGHTS

Joining a peer advisory council can be the answer for you to get to the next level professionally or personally, whatever that definition may mean for you. The benefits are many, regardless of the stage of your business or the season you are in. They are always relevant:

- Have a real connection and high level of trust with your peers.
- It is hard to find other peers who have your back when you need it, who listen when you need it most, and who understand. One member said it best: "My peer council is where I see my best business friends once a month."
- You will not be judged.
- Peers will listen to you openly and seek to understand you. Their feedback is for your best interest, not their best interest. It really is unbiased. And it is in a confidential environment. They are not your "yes" men.
- Reduce stress; increase your positive mind-set.
- Do this by taking time to step away from your business, work on the business, and make progress toward what is important to you.
- Increase clarity and focus.
- Sharing your own experiences reinforces what is going well and where areas of improvement are. The more you talk about the business, the clearer you become.
- Get more ideas and perspectives.
- Hearing what your peers are doing in their own businesses is inspirational. Not everyone thinks the same, and you benefit from other approaches to solving problems or creating opportunities.
- Do more of what you do best.
- By becoming an even better leader and company, you can spend more time on what brings the most value to the company. Therefore, you'll create more success.
- Make connections.

- Be introduced to other peers, whom you share synergies with and who can help you achieve more.
- Learn best practices.
- Learn of resources you were unaware of, best practices, and services or products that can be of benefit.
- Increase the speed of success.
- Each month you have time to work on your business, which allows you to take best-in-class ideas from others whom you trust and who have had the experience and execute them back in the company.
- Make better decisions.
- Be reminded of sound business practices or learn new ones. Find out what you don't know you don't know.

These are just a few reasons that CEOs join peer-to-peer councils. How many of those can you identify with? Whether it's one or two or the whole list of reasons, you can find the fastest, most-rewarding, and most-effective solution by joining a peer advisory group. You might be in business by yourself, but when you have your own peer group, you will never be alone. You'll have your own team of dedicated, experienced, trusted peers, who are ready, willing, and able to share, listen, teach, and support you every step of the way while you do the same for them. You have nothing to lose and everything to gain. Like I said in the Introduction, a peer advisory group is your dream team!

Assignment
Take five minutes right now and do the following exercise. Trust me; it will be the most productive five minutes you will invest in yourself today. Remember, take the time to write it down! It will make a difference.

Envision your future reality.
1. Sit down in a quiet place. Turn your phone off so you have no distractions.

SIT DOWN! SPEAK UP! CASH IN!

2. Take a deep, long breath. Breathe in as much air as you can and hold for three seconds. One thousand one. One thousand two. One thousand three.
3. Exhale slowly.
4. Repeat. Breathe in slowly until your lungs cannot take any more air.
5. Slowly exhale, letting all the air out of your lungs. You should feel significantly more relaxed at this point.
6. Visualize yourself entering a time machine—one that is plush, quiet, and safe. You sit down in a comfy chair and propel yourself into the future.
7. Still relaxed, you land safely. Exit your time capsule and envision your company's office. What do you see? What is going on? What are you doing? What is the environment like? Who else is there? Who is not there? Take in the surroundings and be observant, noticing what you see in the future.
8. Get back in your time capsule and shut the door. You are now traveling back to the present. You arrive safely and open the door to your office.
9. Write down what you experienced. Be specific. How did you feel? How do you feel now? Energized? Surprised? What is different from today? What were you doing? What was your role? What did the company look like? What type of clients did you have?

By relaxing, you were able to clear your mind and envision a different reality than you are currently experiencing. You were able to open your mind to new possibilities. Remember that company of your future? That's the reality you can start creating now. And there is no faster or better way to spur that growth than by turning to a group of your peers. Your peer-to-peer council will help you bridge the gap between your reality today and your future vision. They will have your back and help you get there, while you help them get where they're going, too.

3

Old Dog, New Tricks

Insight: Experience trumps academics

I have never let my schooling interfere with my education. —
Mark Twain, American author and humorist

Now that you're familiar with the general idea of what a peer advisory council is and how it works, it's important to understand that the benefits of participating in such a group exceed even those on the most obvious level. As I said earlier, the value of these organizations percolates into every crevice of your private and professional life. The value is multilevel. It isn't a split-level ranch. You might even think of it as a lighthouse, with a spiral staircase that winds round and round as you make your way to the top. When you get up there, the view is spectacular even on a stormy night, or maybe even especially on a stormy night. You may feel set in your ways. You may feel like you know it all and have all the answers. But the fact is you don't. Joining a peer advisory council will drive that point home far better than I can.

Let's dive deeper into four core concepts that can make all the difference between an average company and one that really shines. As a leader in business, you can't afford to ignore what others have done to climb that winding staircase to the top of the lighthouse. You needn't be an exact follower. In fact, you shouldn't be, but learning from others has and always will be the key to forging your own path to greatness.

Concept 1: Staying Relevant

CEOs can experience a great deal of stress and anxiety, or they can learn to manage it. Joining a peer advisory council is one way to gain the tools to manage effectively the challenges of the job, the changing economy, and the changing needs of their clients, which leads to staying relevant as a company.

Staying relevant means thinking about how your current services and products will be enhanced for the better tomorrow, how they will continue to provide value, and how to gain more market share. Is your industry growing or dying? How is technology changing how you do business or how you should do business? Are you falling behind or leading the way?

CEOs stay awake at night, literally or figuratively, wondering about the future of their businesses, wondering about the answers to the questions above. Unlike hourly employees, you can't just clock in every day, do your job, and trust that it will still be there tomorrow. CEOs know that the responsibility for the company's future falls on their shoulders. To sustain the business today and grow it tomorrow, a CEO has to be relevant to his clients, employees, and vision. It's very difficult for CEOs who are busy working in their business to keep abreast of their clients' needs and changes all around them. CEOs can't let their companies become outdated if they want to serve their customers adequately for another day, another year, or even another decade.

Christy's story is a good example of what I'm talking about when it comes to staying relevant while immersed in a "good old boys" network.

News from the Trenches
Christy can vouch for the need to stay relevant. Christy suddenly and unexpectedly became a third- generation business owner. Her grandfather had started the family-owned business in 1947, and

when he retired, he passed the business on to her father. Christy first started working for the company when she was a teenager. Through the years, she worked her way through several different departments. She learned different areas of the business, never paying too much attention to the way the business ran or why. After all, she wasn't going to run the company one day. She wasn't even sure how long she would work there. Then, unexpectedly, her father passed away, leaving Christy in charge of both the business and her father's and grandfather's legacy.

CEO's definition of relevant:
Sustaining practical value with their customers, employees, and stakeholders.

Christy found herself in unfamiliar territory. She was the first female to head their company in a very male-dominated industry. Plus, Christy had no managerial experience. The business employed senior leaders who thought they could do a better job; some had been working there before Christy was born. Many employees had little faith in Christy's capabilities. Certainly, these were challenges she'd have to face, but there was another issue: the once-prosperous business had flattened in growth. Christy not only had culture challenges to deal with and the legacy of her father to keep alive, but she absolutely had to develop new solutions and ways to compete in a mature industry.

In order to turn things around, Christy needed to be creative and make the company her own. She had to help the company stay relevant and stand out from the competition. So, when her financial advisor recommended a peer council to her, she took action.

When I walked into Christy's office, I saw a beautiful woman in her late twenties seated behind a large desk and surrounded by portraits of her predecessors—her grandfather and father. An opposite wall held a gallery of photos showing the evolution of their products through the years. The office was rich in history; everything in it recalled past successes and growth.

Though her office depicted the past, Christy represented the future, one that was uncertain. She sat behind the same desk and filled the same position as her father, and his father before him, but she knew she couldn't follow the same practices they had. Business as usual wasn't going to work. I could see her determination and feel her energy. Christy made it clear that she wasn't about to let the business fail under her watch. She knew the odds were against her. It's a well-known rule that the first generation starts a business, the second generation runs it, and the third generation ruins it. Christy was determined not to be the generation to ruin it. The main reason family firms fail is that the transfer of leadership is not planned properly, if at all. Usually, the head of the family firm does not officially retire but stays on indefinitely-either because there is no clear heir apparent or no set time frame for retirement. Christy's potential failure rate was probably even higher, given that the transfer of the business was unexpected, and the transition was unplanned.

How Well Do Second and Third Generation Businesses Fare?

According to the Boston-based Family Firm Institute, family businesses that are passed from one generation to the next can expect to see a decline in likely survival rates.

- Only one-third of all family businesses are passed on to the second generation successfully.
- A mere 13 percent of third generation businesses survive.

The Family Firm Institute attributes the high failure rate of multi-generation businesses to a lack of effective planning in the transition of leadership.

It's a well-known rule that the first generation starts a business, the second generation runs it, and the third generation ruins it. Christy was determined not to be the generation to ruin it. The main reason family firms fail is that the transfer of leadership is not planned properly, if at all. Usually, the head of the family firm does not officially retire but stays on indefinitely—either because there is no clear heir apparent or no set time frame for retirement. Christy's potential failure rate was probably even higher, given that the transfer of the business was unexpected, and the transition was unplanned.

A young woman with no management experience has to rise above. Christy knew she would have to make risky decisions. She also never lost sight of the fact that she was solely responsible for protecting her mother's biggest asset and the legacy left by her father and grandfather. She needed an environment where she could be vulnerable—a place where she could surround herself with unbiased peers who would help her develop and implement new initiatives in an old culture.

We talked for a long time in her office, which is part of my company's process in determining the right-fit council for each owner. Learning as much about the owner as possible is critical to proper placement and to be sure he or she would benefit from involvement in a peer advisory council.

Through all the discussion, the last point Christy shared with me was that she knew she needed to overcome odds that weren't in her favor. With a multimillion-dollar company and more than one hundred employees at stake, she needed to share her burden, but there was no way she could do so with her employees or senior managers, nor with her mother or her husband. A peer advisory council afforded her a place to air her concerns and receive the support and insights to make decisions that might not be well received. It provided her with an environment where she could overcome her vulnerability and boost her confidence, without being influenced by naysayers and the statistical probabilities of failure. Above all, her peer advisory council exposed her to new ways to take her relevant mature company into the future.

Two years later, the company won two business awards-the first for being one of the fastest-growing companies in the city and the second for being led by an outstanding president under forty.

Christy's Benefits

- **Culture shift:** Christy had all upper-management positions reevaluated. Job descriptions were updated with expectations.
- **Metrics:** Benchmarks were established for the company and a dashboard created for transparency.
- **Accountability:** Weekly and monthly meetings were instituted to track progress, solve challenges, and measure success.
- **Recognition:** Rewarding for performance through promotions, bonuses, and an annual holiday party created fun and motivation for the team.
- **Communication:** Christy developed techniques to communicate to all employees personally to ensure her message was heard. She instituted a newsletter and vendor days, had employee brown-bag lunches, and spent time in each division every quarter.

How to Stay Relevant in Business

A.J. Foyt, Indy seven-time race-car champion, on how he won so many races: "I get out in front, and I stay out in front."

Staying relevant doesn't mean that the business has to be on the brink of disaster—far from it. The key is that the business has to be proactive, regardless of its current state. It's being aware of what is going on and making sure you're providing something of value to your clients or customers every day. Interacting with peers in different industries is invaluable for learning how to stay relevant. In a council meeting, it is about understanding what changes are happening in their markets and making the connection of how that might impact your industry or your own market. My favorite quote is signed by A. J. Foyt, an unprecedented seven-time championship Indy race-car driver. When asked how he wins so many races, he replied, "I get out in front, and I stay out in front." Staying relevant is about staying competitive and staying out in front. I am forever indebted to Julie Hobson, one of my sales reps back in Los Angeles in the eighties, for getting A. J. to sign that quote for me. I look at it every day as a reminder that I, too, need to stay relevant.

Concept 2: Confidence is King

This may come as a surprise, but the primary responsibility a CEO has to his or her company is not experience or management decisions. The number one responsibility a CEO has to his or her company is to protect the CEO's own confidence. When you join a peer advisory council, the discussions that happen with your peers give your insight into your situation. You realize you are not alone; other CEOs have been there, done that. They have had the experience already. You realize your situation is not insurmountable. A solution is achievable. With clarity you gain a higher level of confidence that you will execute successfully. You are given an injection of possibility beyond what you had before. A high level of confidence is vital to a CEO's clarity, ability to manage, make decisions, and take risks.

What does anything but 100 percent confidence look like? It shows up as a lack of clarity. Fuzzy vision. It shows up as an

> Definition of *Confidence*:
> Arrogance under control

inability to make a decision, lead, or move ahead. If a CEO is not 100 percent confident, leadership suffers and so does performance. Loss of confidence can happen in the snap of a finger. Any hesitation, doubt, or faltering can cause your employees to question your ability to make decisions in line with the company vision. Of course, internally, all CEOs experience a decline in confidence from time to time. Simply put, when you question yourself, others will, too. Tough times require critical decisions, but they come with risks. Personally, you have to have the clarity to make difficult decisions and carry them through. And as a CEO, you have to portray that confidence and strength to your employees, investors, and customers.

Confidence is such an important quality in CEOs that many nonbusiness leaders misconstrue CEOs as having an inflated sense of self-worth. Many people say entrepreneurs, CEOs, and business leaders have big egos and assume they already know everything! Another unfortunate misunderstanding is that the majority of leaders were born confident. Even the most confident leaders do have doubts and fears. But they know how to keep them in check. Financially successful leaders have the luxury of being confident because they've gained clarity on the direction they are taking. They come across as sure of themselves, but not egotistical. It's a level of confidence that must be portrayed, and one that can be categorized as arrogance under control. Achieving that level of confidence and clarity doesn't come automatically, however. It takes work.

Let's take a case in point as an example. Meet Dave! You might say he needed a bit of a confidence booster. Did he get one through a peer advisory group? Well, shall we find out?

News from the Trenches

Dave learned the importance of protecting his confidence and regaining clarity. He and his partner had an established business— one that had been recognized as one of the top places to work in the city and had been named in Inc. Magazine's Annual Top 500/5000 list. A perfect storm had occurred, handing them an onslaught of challenges all at once. As government contractors, they struggled to keep highly skilled, highly paid staff on contract. Not only was it difficult to find the necessary level of talent, but it was also challenging to maintain consistent contracts to keep employees busy.

Dave had been talking about their challenges with his peer advisory council during the last few months. But he was only talking, not really preparing for action. It was summertime and time for their next peer advisory council meeting, which was to be held on one of the member's boats, where they were to meet and have lunch on the Chesapeake Bay. It was a beautiful day, and everyone was enjoying the reprieve—except Dave.

Dave's mind was spinning as he worried about the business. He wasn't sure of anything, especially of himself. The only thing Dave wanted to do on this beautiful day was complain. On top of their challenges with finding and keeping skilled employees, a big government contract had just been postponed, creating a significant cash-flow problem, and one of their key employees had a long-term illness. Plus, he'd just been informed by their accounting firm of an upcoming accounting-rule change that was going to be costly. Dave was visibly worried. Dave questioned his leadership and wondered how all of this could have happened. He ran the business conservatively, had great success, won awards, and planned ahead. Yet here he was, in big trouble.

Dave's mind-set was about as low as it could go. So, when it came time to discuss business, Dave let loose. He complained about his frustrations to the point of whining. He had no lack of problems. To Dave, the meeting was an opportunity to vent. He was a few minutes in when one of his peers stood up and set Dave straight. The peer reminded Dave that he could either whine about his problems all day or pull up his bootstraps and do something about it. Giving it to him straight, he told Dave it could be worse—there could be yellow tape across his business's front door, indicating it had been shut down. Dave could have the same yellow tape across the door of his home once the bank foreclosed on it. If that happened, Dave would put his employees' livelihoods, his family's security, and his intended legacy at risk. Plus, he'd be humiliated that the entire community witnessed his failure. Thankfully, Dave's peer reminded him that getting back in the saddle was essential; he had to find a way to keep his company alive. To avoid losing everything, Dave needed renewed confidence.

This honest lecture was exactly what Dave really needed to hear. He had been so caught up in his problems that he had forgotten he could turn things around. He'd lost sight of the fact that others were relying on him and he had to be the leader everyone needed, expected, and relied on to navigate these turbulent issues. Dave's peer advisory council members helped him realize that he had what it takes to get his business back on track. They helped him get clear on what steps needed to be taken. After all, if he had the confidence to start his business in the first place, he also had the confidence to get his dream back.

Dave's worries had him caught up in his emotions. He was losing momentum rather than finding solutions. It took the straightforward and unbiased words of his peer advisory council to make him realize what he needed to do. If someone outside of his peer council had told him the same thing, Dave probably wouldn't have taken it to heart. There was no way anyone outside of his peer group could understand what he was going through. Luckily, Dave's peer advisory council members did understand what he was going through. They knew what was at risk and how it felt to know everything was on the line. That's why their advice was so valuable—and why Dave heeded it immediately. As his peer advisory council members had said, Dave had no alternative. He had to change his attitude and get his "arrogance" back.

Dave's Benefit

- Confidence: It was that simple. Dave just needed to hear other leaders knew he could do it. He trusted them; he knew they had his best interests at heart and had been there too. He just needed a little encouragement to get back on track, a reality check.

When you find yourself quietly questioning if you are doing the right thing, taking the right actions, choosing the right strategy, or making the right decision, it's important to find a support network that will help you develop clarity and confidence. Clarity is

> "Councils are really the avenue that give leaders the confidence and clarity to do what they know they need to do."
> — Jeff, Attorney, VA

essential when embarking on a new path, whether you're developing a new product, entering a new market, or even creating a strategic partnership. Your conviction and leadership need to be at their peak during those times. Your peer council is the safe haven where you can get an extra dose of clarity to make tough decisions and execute them successfully.

Concept 3: The Right Kind of Advice

The number one-person CEOs listen to for business feedback and perspective isn't his or her managers or employees. It isn't his or her brother-in-law or close friends. It's fellow business leaders. The most important person a CEO can listen to is his or her peers. Sure, a CEO can consider the advice and opinions of others, but his or her peers are the most trustworthy group for providing valuable business advice, the right kind of advice.

Business leaders work hard to maximize performance. They go to great depths to get the right people, processes, and policies in place. But unfortunately, many of the efforts taken to improve employee performance are misplaced. Business leaders set accountability standards for their employees and supervisors. Those are good things, but they will produce only adequate performance.

If business leaders want exceptional performance from their supervisors and staff, they must implement peer accountability. Business leaders must hold more than their

> You decide the level of your involvement in your company.

employees accountable; they must also hold themselves accountable. Do you remember Bill, the construction company CEO who was having problems with his project manager? Bill could either ignore the continual problems this manager caused or he could make other choices. Bill had to hold himself accountable before holding Todd accountable. As long as he let Todd manage the client process poorly, Bill would keep experiencing the same setbacks. In this case, it was Bill—not his project manager—who should first be held accountable. Bill's choices were the cause of his problems. Until he did something about them, those problems would plague him endlessly.

Having peers who hold you accountable for your decisions and actions is the most productive way to create change. Peer council meetings are the one place where a CEO can turn to someone who gets it and even calls him or her out

> Other leaders are the only ones who truly understand the impact of problems and successes of an owner.

when appropriate. That's what happened when Dave's peer advisory council member called him out and told him to stop whining and do something to change his business's trajectory. Sometimes business leaders need a reality check from a trusted colleague who can remind him or her where the ultimate responsibility lies.

Because your peers are equal and are also business leaders who are not competitors, you'll respect their opinions and trust their experience. Unlike your relationships with others, you can't make excuses with your peers. They know better, and you know they know better. It's why peer advisory councils work so well and why leaders who really want to progress turn to peer advisory councils. These leaders seek accountability—from themselves. It's too easy for them to make excuses and justify their actions (or lack thereof). Someone needs to push them to reach their potential.

Consider this: all professional athletes have coaches who hold them accountable for their self-discipline, workout, diet, practices, daily habits, commitment, and improvement. Athletes are constantly pushed to accept responsibility for their performance. As a CEO, you are no different. Your coaches are your peer-to-peer council members. They hold you accountable for your performance and your reality when it comes to your company. They are the mirror that helps you see things more clearly, letting you know exactly where the buck stops. Everybody needs someone to push them, especially business leaders, who aren't necessarily accountable to anyone.

> As an owner, you are the professional athlete of your business. Who is your coach?

One peer council member, Debbie, was so dedicated to holding herself accountable that she even warned her council members that she couldn't be trusted when she said a certain phrase. Debbie said, "If I ever nod and say, 'I will try that,' I'm lying. I will not try that. It just means that I'm listening, soaking it all in, but I'm not going to try it. That promise is just lip service. Therefore, when I say I'll try, I need you, my peers, to call me out on it. What I need to say is, 'I will do that,' not 'I will try that.'" Debbie was honest about her sometime lack of accountability. She leaned on her peers, asking them to demand a status report from her at the start of every meeting.

Peer advisory council members often admit that they wouldn't have tried new ideas if they knew their fellow members wouldn't follow up. Having to share with council members regularly is a powerful incentive for business leaders to keep their word. Janet's story illustrates my point.

News from the Trenches
Janet's story reveals what can happen if you don't have a peer level of accountability. When Janet walked into her monthly advisory council meeting, it was obvious her mind-set was very low. Her walk was sluggish, and her head was hanging. She bottomed out at a— 1. The entire council was concerned. In all our council meetings, we facilitate the entire meeting process. One of our processes is to have the members go through their My Transition™; this is a tool in the

meetings that I elaborate on in chapter 2.

Janet sat down and then shared her story. Janet owned a family-run antenna business that employed her relatives and many employees who were related to each other—brother and sister, husband and wife, mother and daughter. Janet had more than fifty employees to look after, and so far, business had been steady. Janet had been a member of her peer advisory council for years. She had always been forthcoming and brought great ideas to the table. That's why the members were so surprised when she shared her news.

Two weeks earlier, Janet had hired her first chief operating officer. The news shocked her peers because she hadn't mentioned it in any of the previous meetings—not even the thought of hiring a COO. Janet didn't think it was a big deal. The opportunity had come suddenly with a good friend of theirs. He recently was out of work, and he seemed like a perfect fit. Janet hired him quickly before he could accept another offer. He started immediately.

Janet told her peers what happened the day before the council meeting. While driving to the office, she received a call from her banker, who asked if she was sitting down. When she told him she was driving, he asked her to pull over—this was serious. Apprehensive and curious, Janet obliged. Her banker then told her that the bank was calling her $200,000 line of credit. Dumbfounded, Janet asked what he was referring to. He explained that she tripped one of the covenants in their agreement by purchasing $200,000 worth of purchase orders.

Janet told her banker she'd get back to him and hung up the phone. She was in disbelief as she drove to the office. The new COO was her trusted friend. She hired him quickly and didn't think she needed to put any financial controls in place. The new COO had placed more than $200,000 of non-cancelable purchase orders for future product—with no permission from her. That mistake was not the COO's fault; Janet hadn't bothered to give him guidelines or training. Now she had a $200,000 bank note to pay, $200,000 worth of *purchase orders to pay, and no cash flow from the inventory—and she could not return the product. The company was in critical financial distress. Because she didn't hold her new COO accountable, Janet had to lay off half of her staff members, who were like family to her. Ultimately, though, she was the one who was accountable for his actions.*

Jane's Benefit

- You don't know what you don't know: Janet learned what she didn't know in setting up proper controls for a key position. The other members of her council were reminded of the importance of vetting out new ideas, positions, ventures, and so on, as they can be the most risky and costly if not executed well.

> "This has become a valuable resource for many of my business decisions. It has saved me thousands of dollars in just my first year of membership."
> -Larry, Convenient Store Franchise, MD

Janet could have avoided this devastating scenario by approaching her peer advisory council before she made a major hiring decision. During our orientation, new peer council members are told to seek their peers' advice when embarking on anything new—including hiring for a new position, researching a new market, designing a new product, or entering a new partnership. If Janet had sought her peers' advice, she might not have been saddled with so much debt and regret.

Concept 4: The Best Kind of Confidentiality

When it comes to peer councils, confidentiality cannot be overrated. Confidentiality is black and white; it can have no gray areas or blurred lines. It is also the foundation that every CEO needs in order to be honest. There can be no exceptions—ever.

"What you see here, what you say here, what you hear here, let it stay here when you leave here" is imperative to the success of every peer advisory council. To be effective, there can be no outside discussions about the other members of the council or the content of the meetings. Confidentiality cannot be compromised in any way. It is an impenetrable shield that creates the trust necessary for CEOs and business leaders to be candid, honest, and vulnerable. Without it, bad advice will be given because key data are missing or withheld due to fear. The result can be devastating to the outcome of a problem.

There is no other place CEOs can be vulnerable. They can't express their fears, doubts, or concerns with advisors, customers, employees, competitors, or investors. A peer advisory council meeting is the only place that CEOs can be totally honest and open without the fear of being judged, belittled, criticized, ridiculed, or worse—having their innermost feelings and thoughts become the talk of the town.

Our peer advisory council members adhere to the highest level of confidentiality. They cannot comment about another member, even when prodded to do so. They don't go home and share each other's stories with their spouses, friends, or coworkers. One hundred percent confidentiality makes peer advisory councils effective.

News from the Trenches

John had only been to four peer advisory council meetings when he mentioned that he was creating a succession plan. John was in his early sixties and felt he needed to address the effects on his business if something were to unexpectedly happen to him. He wanted to ensure that his company's future would be in good hands for the sake of his wife and his employees. John had only known the members of his peer advisory council for a short time, but he trusted them implicitly. He asked his peers to take on the highly trusted role as temporary advisors to his wife if he became unable to run the company.

John had contemplated his decision extensively, but the answer came to him easily. He explained to his fellow peer advisory council members that they were the ones who knew him best and whom he trusted to do the right thing for his wife and family, his business, and his employees. He'd only known them for four short months, and he met them only once a month. But John had no apprehension about leaving his legacy in their care. He passed over his accountant, attorney, and senior managers as the bearers of his legacy. John's faith rested with this peer group, who had earned his full trust and confidence.

John's Benefit

- Trusted advisors: Your peer advisory council will become your trusted advisors so much that you will trust them to take care of your interests if needed in time of emergency.

Stories such as John's are not uncommon. While I don't often hear CEOs ask council members to carry out their wishes in the event of incapacitation, I often hear members say that their council members are not only trusted advisors, but also "their very best friends that they see only once a month."

By being involved in a peer-to-peer council, CEOs realize there are no secrets to business success. In reality, the secret is having a group of

> *"You know you are in the right council for you when you feel your fellow council peers are the very best friends you see only once a month."*
> *- Art, Manufacturing Paper Products, KS*

peers that you can trust with your biggest asset and your legacy— peers you can feel free to confide in, be vulnerable around, and trust to hold you accountable. Your council members will learn your priorities, wishes, and fears so well that you can trust them above anyone else to step into your shoes and do the right thing for your family, your employees, and your legacy.

INSIGHTS

- Making a decision to join a peer advisory council is both tangible and intangible. Ultimately, what is peace of mind worth to you? I think it's probably worth its weight in gold!
- Personal growth unleashes potential.
- Because you are surrounded by peers, you will naturally be challenged to up your game. It is no different than when adults indicate the change in them when they have children. Your peers will do the same in business. It is your catalyst to opening up more possibilities within you and your team. It is your way to get beyond the same old thing and gain more momentum toward your goals.
- Confidence breeds clarity.
- The more elevated your confidence, the greater your ability to execute, make decisions, see opportunities, and tackle the unknown.
- Relevance makes a company remarkable.
- Taking time to reflect and finesse what will make your company unique will happen in your council meetings. It is one way to stay innovative and ahead of your competitors.
- Bridge the gap between reality and your future.
- A common concept is that what got you to where you are won't get you where you want to go. Joining a council will enable you to see the possibilities of what needs to happen differently and empower you to make it happen.
- Confidentiality generates productive vulnerability.
- Your council is a safe haven, a place that is your place.
- Accountability comes from peers alone.
- The type and level of accountability are personal. You decide. Regardless of the level, it exists on a level that is professional and motivating. It creates energy.
- Peer business leaders have the CEO's ear.
- Who do you respect most? Other CEOs. You have their ear and they have yours. It's mutual sharing of experiences for the greater good of the group that leads to exponential results. It's the right kind of advice.

4

FINDING THE RIGHT COUNCIL

Insight: ROI = return on your involvement.

The best vision is insight. - Malcolm Forbes, Publisher, Forbes Magazine

Peer-to-peer councils are not all created equal. Each is unique, contributing varying levels of experience, professions, and personalities to the team. If you're interested in joining a peer-to- peer council, it's important to know what to look for in order to get your highest ROI—return on involvement. Participating in the right group will enable you to feel you are spending your time wisely, that you connect on a business level with the peers involved, and that you can relate to them and them to you. When you are in the right group, it is effortless; it is energizing because you are learning and making progress faster than you have before. Your goal is to join a group that makes you feel as though it's your personal group of advisors.

Let's take a close look at the things you should look for as you search for the peer advisory council that best matches your needs. Obviously, we'll need to start with how to find a group!

Search Sources

One question I often get is how to find a peer-to-peer group or council. Traditionally they aren't advertised in newspapers and on the radio, but they are available. With a little research, you can locate them in your area. Follow these steps during your search.

1. Search the web. Search for peer groups, peer advisory groups, or peer councils in your area.
2. Consult with local professionals. Talk to your accountant, attorney, banker, advisors, or other professionals who may know of groups or councils in your area.
3. Contact local business organizations or associations. Business organizations, chambers of commerce, local business journal organizations, and corresponding publications in your area may have information about peer groups or councils. They could help introduce you to some- one with the connections or information you seek.

The Right Questions

EXAMPLE QUESTIONS ARE LISTED AS A GUIDE.

- Verify their longevity and mission as a company or individual who creates and moderates peer advisory councils.
- How long have they been in the business?
- Why did they go into this business?
- What is their vision with the business?
- What does success mean to them?
- Ask about the credentials of the moderator.
- What business experience does the moderator have?
- How did the moderator become trained and skilled in leading a council meeting?
- How long has he or she been moderating?
- Determine why there is an opening on the council.
- Why did someone leave?
- What has turnover been like, and why has it occurred over the last six months to a year?
- What is the number of leaders in the group today, and what is the desired number?
- Have they ever been at the desired number of members?

If not, why not?
- What is their philosophy on running a council meeting?
- Is the meeting structured or free-flowing?
- Ask for a sample meeting agenda.
- What processes do they use to create value for the members?
- How do the members get value?
- Where, when, how frequent, and what is the length of the meetings?
- Are speakers or education of some sort involved in the meeting?
- How often can I ask the other members a question to get their perspective and insight from their experiences?
- What are my obligations as a member?
- How long is my membership?
- What are the expectations of a member?
- What happens if I don't like the first meeting or some of the members?
- Determine where the synergies exist between you and the other CEOs on the council.
- How do I know these are truly peers of mine?
- Who are the members? What do they do?
- Understand their policy and procedures.
- Can members do business with each other?
- Are there times they socialize with each other?
- What happens if you miss a meeting?
- What happens if you are late or need to leave early?
- If you have a business partner, what happens if you want your partner to attend a meeting?
- How is confidentiality handled and enforced?
- Is there any accountability to the CEO in the meeting?

Your council experience will depend on the services you seek and the individuals or organizations that offer them. Finding a peer-to-peer group or council company that diligently and carefully works to ensure a good match among your fellow peers and the council is crucial. They should be taking the time to get to know you and you to know them. Choose a council considering your needs and your experience by referring to your answers in the Determining a Right-Fit Council checklist in the appendix. Also, choose a council that is structured to evolve to support continual growth over time. Then you can pursue a dream team, your future council, which will become integral to your success.

The All-Important Moderator

At the head of each group is the moderator. Let's take a close look at the moderator's role in the council.

A recent Kansas City Star Business Journal article discussed five problems with high-level peer groups. After reading it, I agreed with the author that many peer groups overpromise and under-deliver. When peer groups under-deliver, however, it can usually be attributed to flaws in the council model or the moderator's leadership.

In a typical council model, the moderator has three job responsibilities. He or she is usually the marketer, the sales executive, who also sells the members and the moderator.

In other words, the person who markets, sells, and delivers the product is one and the same. It's unheard of in business to find one person who can carry out all three responsibilities and do them each well. It's akin to spinning plates, starting with the plate of the marketer, then setting up and spinning the sales plate, and keeping both of them spinning steadily while adding a third plate, the moderator. Few people have the skills to keep all three plates, or roles in this case, spinning at the same pace. All three responsibilities require three entirely different areas of expertise and training.

Consider this example I use often when explaining the

difference between marketing, selling, and moderating: I grew up in a small, rural farming community known as the Goose Capital of the World. Each year, thousands of geese flocked to our area while migrating south from Canada for the winter. There were duck blinds everywhere in the harvested corn and soybean fields, with duck decoys spread all around. Hunters sat in their duck blinds, waiting for the geese to be lured in by the duck decoys and land.

In this example, the duck decoys are marketing and the hunters are sales. Marketing lures prospects and selling "kills" them. As you can see, marketing has a different function than sales, and both of these are very different from moderating. The moderator is responsible for creating the experience. Moderators are the ones who deliver the service—after marketing and sales have turned prospects into clients.

Definition of Marketing and Sales Using the Goose-Hunting Analogy:

Marketing = luring in the geese with duck decoys

Sales = the hunter shooting the geese

As a CEO, wouldn't it be great to hire only one person who could do everything? Some might think so. That person would be a rare find, and he or she would also be indispensable and worth his or her weight in gold. Chances are that even a capable person attempting to do three diverse jobs would create challenges for a business.

People who attempt three roles are usually stronger in one. If they happen to be strong in moderating, but not in sales, the result will be a weak mix of council members. Regardless of his or her strength, a person's inevitable shortcomings will weaken the council. The model simply is not scalable and fails to deliver good service.

Sometimes peer-group membership is misaligned. A person filling all three roles is likely to be more concerned about making the sale than taking the time to find the new member who is the right fit for the entire council. A person's time is limited when he or she is doing all three roles. The salesperson's priorities will naturally lean toward sales because he or she makes money by closing a new member sooner rather than later. As a result, many times at the expense of filling a seat that is not filled by the best member choice possible.

Unfortunately, seller-marketer-moderators often sell new members who are not a good fit either for their specific councils or with the council concept in general. The misplaced member will likely leave because he or she doesn't believe he or she is getting value from participation. When the salesperson is also the moderator, the mind-set is, "That's okay—I'll just go out and find someone else to fill his or her spot." Unfortunately, that will fill the empty chair, but it won't address the greater problem of an inferior service that fails to meet the expectations or needs of its current members.

In the peer group business, customers know each other, and they know that the value they receive from their council depends on the quality of the members. Misaligned membership or membership that falls short of expectations will affect the value every member receives.

Helpful hint: When choosing a peer group, consider the experience and expertise of the moderator before making a decision to join.

The objective is to learn from and respect the group members, and their objective is to benefit from your feedback. Your background, experience, challenges, strengths, and weaknesses should help you determine the right fit for your council. If you join a council that has not been vetted, you'll feel uncomfortable among the group and will not get the value you expect and need from your participation. A reputable and experienced peer council company will make sure the moderator and members are vetted and aligned in order for the relationships to be advantageous to all.

The Role of the Moderator

Another fundamental issue arises when the person running the meetings does not have moderator experience. Moderating requires unique skills, which are often the opposite of the sales and marketing skills. The moderator has to have a high degree of business acumen. This is our number one skill when screening for the right-fit moderator. The more moderators know about business, the better they will moderate. In my company, all our moderators are past business leaders or held large P&L responsibility. The reason for that is they will understand how to subtly lead the direction of a conversation and see opportunities when they arise. What you don't want is the conversation held by the peers to be above the head of the moderator.

The moderator's ego is checked at the door. The moderator has already had career success and does not need to prove his or her worth. Moderator egos can override moderators' roles, making the meeting about them—while the real purpose takes a backseat. Instead of guiding, they become pompous, showing that they have all of the answers. Acting as a consultant, they run the meetings, often believing their advice is better than that of the members.

The moderator with a consulting background has to be careful to separate the role of moderator from consultant while facilitating the group meeting. The consultant role doesn't have a place in a peer advisory council meeting. Because consultants would be in a position to solicit member services, there would be a conflict of interest with the members.

Good listening skills are also very important. This is essential to hearing what is really going on with the conversation versus what it appears to be on the surface.

Diplomacy and tact are key to the moderator's success. This is the number two skill we screen for. The moderator has to have the ability to manage tactfully leaders who are talking too much, rambling, not talking, or stray off course, and change direction when needed. Without diplomacy and tact, the meeting can run amuck.

There are many more skill sets, but these are the top skill sets to screen for.

Don't underestimate the importance of the moderator. My philosophy of the moderator role is based on the *Tao of Leadership*, which states that a moderator is one whose presence within the group is acknowledged by the group and whose actions are mostly transparent to the group. True moderators quietly encourage open dialogue, while gently directing the group's dialogue toward leadership growth and personal learning.

What does the success of a good moderator look like? Imagine a meeting in which all members gain new insight that they can put to practical use in their business. Some might call them epiphanies or aha moments, and they are common in properly moderated peer councils. When moderators guide the group to challenge its perspectives, good solutions arise.

Helpful hint: A skilled moderator guides without being pushy.

A skilled moderator is so good that it can appear that he or she isn't moderating at all. It might seem that moderators have minimal involvement when they are so adept that they fulfill their role without domination. Good moderators interject only to keep the dialogue on track, provide clarity, and when it's necessary to facilitate the process to everyone's benefit. Rather than following an agenda, good moderators follow a purpose. More important, they do not attempt to impress, but as a result of doing their job well, they are very impressive.

Just as important is knowing what a moderator does not do. A moderator does not direct toward his or her own agenda, engage his or her ego in a conversation, outcome, or situation, or manipulate a

> The right moderator does not attempt to impress, but as a result of doing his or her job well, he or she is impressive.

process. Inside a meeting, the moderator is not a coach, advisor, mentor, or consultant. You might say that a moderator is really a facilitator. He or she knows how to get a lively and meaningful conversation going among members of the group. The focus is group-directed. The moderator is merely the guide as the council members grow and change within the group. There are four stages of growth and change that the moderator must account for.

Stage 1: The first stage is when members feel most connected to the person who introduced them to the group. The council member, John, says to a fellow CEO, "Bob, I am a member of Example Council—you may know Tina, who put the group together." If John positions his relationship in terms of the moderator or the person who "sold" him into the group, he is still aligned with an individual rather than the entire council group.

Stage 2: In the second stage, the member will identify less with one person and more with the council. For example, John might say, "Bob, meet Bill; he and I are in the same council." There is more leadership in relating to specific members of the group.

Stage 3: The third stage is the level where members claim leadership of the council, that is, my peer council, our meeting, my fellow members, and so on. In John's case, he might say, "Bob, meet Bill; he is in my council." In this stage, members grow to view their council members as their own personal advisors.

Stage 4: The fourth, ultimate stage is the state that every moderator should encourage his or her members to reach—it is the level where members integrate their council experience into the fabric of their company. The council becomes a necessary component to the company's strategic plan, strategy for success, and CEO's development. Their council is an extension of their team.

How does a moderator learn how to guide meeting discussions effectively? Has the moderator received training? Every business owner should ask these questions before joining a peer advisory council. There should be no doubt that the moderator has the very best interest of the council's members at heart. Skilled moderators are not solely motivated by money—they do it for the satisfaction of being involved in an environment where others succeed.

Yes, problems can arise within peer-to-peer councils. But those problems are avoidable if the peer advisory council company has the right people in the right roles, if there are no conflicts of interest, if the motivation behind each role is geared toward the best outcome for its members, and if the council members are equally matched. When those pieces fit perfectly, the members—not the moderators—become the leaders of their council. They become connected as they become an integral component of it and the success of its members. It's the ultimate level, one that every peer-to-peer council should aspire to.

What is the difference among all of these roles? A good analogy is their role in teaching you to ride a bike.

- The **coach** encourages your desire and inspires you to ride a bike and ride it better.
- The **mentor** shares with you his or her experience/expertise of riding a bike.
- The **consultant** studies the mechanics of riding the bike, teaches you, and then leaves you to continue to ride the bike.
- The **advisor** knows the mechanics of the bike, tells you, and then leaves you to ride the bike on your own.
- The **moderator** facilitates the experience with you and others to ensure you learn all the aspects of riding a bike.

Definitions:

- The **coach** asks thorough questions to get to the root of the matter. He or she does not give answers but creates aha moments by helping clients find answers themselves.
- The **mentor** is someone who has done what the mentee hopes to accomplish. Been there, done that. He or she shares stories of his or her experiences.
- The **consultant** gives guidance as an expert. He or she typically has some responsibility or task to accomplish and may or may not pass knowledge onward.
- The **advisor** gives advice without owning any actions. He or she has real-world experience.
- The **moderator** facilitates the meeting and creates the environment for the members to act like coaches with each other.

Coaching versus Moderating

Many peer organizations offer coaching to supplement the peer council experience. It's important to decide whether you want both services. Does the moderator have the training necessary to act as a coach? Often, moderators have no training in executive coaching. It's also important to understand the types of services you can receive and how they differ.

The Moderator Facilitates the Following:

- Members gain clarity of what the CEO wants/needs from peers when processing a COPI.
- The member presenting talks 20 percent of the time and listens 80 percent while others analyze and dissect the question.
- Avoids having other members hijacking the issue and making it their own.
- Avoids solutions being presented too quickly.
- Ensures others do not interject or ask questions until a CEO completes his or her question.

Now that you know the definition of each professional career role, let's break down the categories. There are different types of coaches, for instance. To coach properly an individual must be trained in coaching techniques. Also, there are subcategories of coaching, such as life coaching, executive coaching, and career coaching. If your peer council includes coaching, you will have to know the type of coaching offered, the purpose of the coaching, and whether the individual is qualified to coach you. Sometimes coaching helps you gain clarity, prepare for your council meeting, or implement or execute your goals, or sometimes it simply provides support. Sometimes coaching is more involved, and in those cases, the coach must have the credentials. If you are paying for coaching services, make sure the coach has the credentials to provide the level of service you deserve.

Coaching years ago, acquired a negative stigma, because coaching was perceived as a last resort for corporate leaders to develop into satisfactory employees or be fired. Today, however, coaching is viewed as a good investment for top performers.

Because of the different skills required, it can be difficult to find a trained, qualified coach who can also succeed as a moderator. If that is the case, a CEO will have to determine if he or she needs both, or just one of those services.

> **Questions to Ask the Moderator when Considering Being Part of That Council:**
>
> - Are you trained to moderate?
> - What is your professional background? How well do you understand business from an owner's perspective?
> - Why have you chosen to moderate peer councils versus consulting or coaching, or are you doing both?
> - What is your philosophy on coaching and having coaching credentials?
> - What is your definition of a well-run meeting?

If the moderator and the coach are the same, the individual has to be disciplined enough to not create a conflict of interest, which creates a barrier to trust. Conflict of interest exists because of the following:

- The coach has to be careful the member does not bring up topics in the coaching session that should be reserved for the council meeting. Topics where diverse experience and insights are needed are best suited to a council setting. If discussed with a coach, there is only one opinion and perspective given.

- If a member needs quick feedback on a pressing issue, it can be difficult for a coach to ask the member to wait until the next council meeting. Of course, an alternative is for the coach to suggest the member contact the council outside of the meeting for perspectives if time is of the essence. The key is for the council to become the first source of feedback, not the coach. Otherwise, the member primarily bonds with the coach versus the council for the answers he or she seeks. I have seen this numerous times; it's hard for one person to serve a client as the coach and the moderator.

- Many times, the coach can assume the role of a consultant. When a member brings up a topic that is a challenge, opportunity, problem, or idea, the coach cannot use the same process used in a council meeting as a moderator, because there are no other members to ask clarifying questions and give feedback. The coach then takes on or assumes that role. One head is not as good as ten council members sitting around a table, so it's easy for coaches to start consulting while trying to bridge that gap.

Be thoughtful when evaluating whether your moderator can also be your coach. Just because the moderator may have the skill set doesn't mean trust will not be compromised.

The Process in the Meetings

One fundamental but subtle difference among peer advisory councils is how they refer to themselves. Some identify as "groups," while others call themselves "councils." Others identify as advisory boards or groups. To a CEO, the title might not matter. Philosophically, however, there is more to a name than meets the eye.

"Group" is an informal term that defines a gathering of people, perhaps for a specific purpose—for example, an advisory group for the purpose of giving advice. By definition, however, a council is a group of people who come together for consultation, deliberation, or discussion. I prefer the term "council," because it best defines the purpose—for peer advisory council members to receive different insights and perspectives from the experience of fellow members. Peer-to-peer companies shouldn't offer professional advice inside the peer meeting, and CEOs shouldn't seek professional advice from a peer-to-peer council. That is what professionals are for. Councils offer educated and experienced feedback based on a particular situation or circumstance. It's real-life experiences.

"Group" simply indicates that people have come together. Unfortunately, it fails to identify the purpose. Councils, on the other hand, specifically define that purpose. It's part of the philosophy behind the process.

To ensure longevity and value for a CEO within a peer-to-peer council, there must be structure. A business owner's time is too valuable to dedicate to a group that lacks vision as to how it will help a CEO achieve the next level.

Are You Wowed?

One CEO who was referred to me, Martha, had a dissatisfying experience as a member of a competing peer group. I called her to learn why she was considering leaving her group. Why did she want to speak with me? When I posed the question to her, a lengthy hesitation followed, along with some obvious struggling as she attempted to find the best way to word her response. Finally, she said, "The only way I know to explain this to you, Tina, is that I'm looking for a wow experience."

Without asking her definition of a "wow experience," I got it. I immediately understood what she meant. "What you're saying is that you want to walk out of a meeting and have gained so much value that you say, 'That was worth my time today. Of all the other things I could have done, this was the best use of my time.'" Martha didn't need an experience that literally knocked her socks off, but she did want to leave her meetings convinced that the time spent was worthwhile.

Martha became a member in one of my councils and remained one for years. She attributes her rise in satisfaction to the structure of the meetings she attended. Structure is the only way to ensure that members like Martha walk away with valuable insights every time. Without a process, it's always a gamble.

My Transition

During years of facilitating meetings, I've observed that CEOs have sometimes taken twenty, thirty, even sixty minutes to settle in. Some remained in tactical mode, addressing their daily responsibilities, putting out last-minute fires, even taking one last phone call. Within a four-hour meeting, even twenty minutes is too much time to waste. The transition time had to be shortened. It's analogous to going on vacation. How many days does it take before you assume the vacation mind-set? Suddenly you only have a few days left. How much better could your experience be if you were in vacation mode on day one?

I've learned that a quick adoption of the right mind-set has a positive correlation to a member's overall meeting experience. I call this transition MyTransition™. It's used by members to transition quickly from their tactical mind-set to a more strategic mind-set in which they work on rather than in the business. It's difficult to change perspectives when your mind is still on business as usual. CEOs go through a brief, but effective and intentional, exercise before each meeting that transitions them from their roles in their businesses to a strategic one that gives them a quick analysis and dashboard of where they currently are in their business. If your council does not have this process, you can do it alone on the way to your meeting. Here's how.

Rank on a scale of 1 (low) to 10 (high) how you are doing with the following:
➢ Personal life (because personal impacts you as a leader in the business)
➢ Health (because excellent health is required for peak CEO performance)
➢ How impactful is the least performing area on the business
➢ Where are you needed that adds the most value to the company
➢ How is your net margin (is it trending up, down or stable)

➤ What's the level of energy and passion you are exhibiting in the business

Now answer what it will take to make them a 10.

Each month you can ask yourself any questions you need. The key is to open your mind to broader thinking before walking into the meeting. Thanks to a little preplanning, you will become engaged and with the right mind-set within minutes versus an hour or more.

> *"One of the problems with many organizations is that they get into 'me speak,' but, with the Council, you get a [very] different focus and grounding that gives you an alternative way of thinking about things."*
>
> *- Billy, Packaging Company, MD*

The difference between an excellent council and a mediocre one can also be attributed to processes, all of which are designed to be result—and value-oriented. Vet your council, making sure that it does not meet for the sake of meeting, but rather meets so that each member benefits from his or her participation. Other processes ensure that the appropriate challenging questions are presented and that members can transfer their thoughts into actions. I call this technique the Business Accelerator™. The key for members is to capture thoughts and desired actions throughout the meeting. Then, before the meeting ends, identify the actions that can benefit you most first. This simple step can ensure clarity.

What's in it for You?

After identifying a peer advisory council that matches your needs and objectives, you vetted the moderator and the members of the group. You also determined whether or not you wanted to avail yourself of coaching services. Next, you have to ask what the group can do for you. Naturally, you've already given the matter some thought. Otherwise, you wouldn't have looked for a peer advisory group in the first place. However, let's dig deeper now.

In each peer-to-peer council meeting, CEOs can present their unique challenges, opportunities, problems, and ideas, which I shorten to COPI. It's a thoughtful process that helps members move beyond obstacles and explore the viability of business opportunities. Within the peer- to-peer council, the members follow a method as they present a COPI. This is a key concept you've got to embrace as you go into the peer advisory council. You're there to probe your challenges, maximize opportunities, solve problems, and hatch new ideas that will help propel your company to even greater success. Regardless of the topic, members must clearly present and reveal why it's important to them. They also need to reveal what they've done in the past, what they are considering doing, and what they want their peers to address. It's one way to make sure all members understand the issue and what is being asked of them. It requires thought, consideration, and preparation on the CEO's part, but it helps CEOs to define their needs, which is necessary for gaining the desired type of insights from their peers. The process gives the CEO clarity about his or her situation. CEOs learn that the challenge or opportunity is sometimes not what they originally perceived it to be. For the best results, a CEO should define his or her issue before the meeting; however, the process can be done during the meeting as well.

The COPI process is all about structure, which prevents valuable time from being wasted. Members should spend 20 percent of their time talking and 80 percent of their time listening. Valuable meeting time should not be wasted because a CEO is unsure what he or she wants from his or her peers. The other members should not have to waste their time with needless questions to understand the issue at hand.

A highly functional peer-to-peer council is well-organized.

While a council member is speaking or posing a question, no one should interject or ask questions. Interruptions pull the member's presentation off course, and eventually the entire meeting can lose its structure.

Once the CEO has exhausted all points in his or her COPI (challenge, opportunity, problem, or idea) presentation, his or her peers ask questions for clarity. At this stage, members should refrain from trying to solve the problem. Solving too early often results in poor advice given because conclusions and assumptions were made before all the data were presented. After all questions have been asked, the members take a few moments to quietly develop their recommendations. Only then do the members share their thoughts. Sometimes recommendations invite further questions. That's perfectly fine: it often raises other considerations that bring further clarity to the issue.

The Presentation of a COPI.

- The member presents the topic.
- The member presents why it's important.
- The member explains past actions taken.
- The member explains future actions considered.
- The member provides relevant background.
- The member informs the group of what is being requested of them, that is, insight, solutions, or just listening.
- Questions from council members follow to gain clarity.
- Members share experiences, suggestions, ideas, and solutions.
- Members gain further clarity, if needed.

Once the process is complete, the member posing the question considers the feedback and whether he or she wants to use all or part of it, or a combination to solve his or her problem or opportunity.

Reflection and Accountability

Just as it is important for a CEO to transition from the day-to-day tactical mind-set to a strategic one, it's just as important for the CEO to reflect on the value he or she received from the meeting and how it can benefit his or her business. Reflection helps business leaders define their next steps before the upcoming meeting. Thinking about the meeting can enable them to set attainable goals while also introducing them to the concept of accountability—which is one of the main reasons CEOs join a peer group.

As previously noted, accountability is expected in peer advisory councils—regardless of type. Accountability occurs at different levels, depending

> In a council meeting:
> We tell stories
> because the truth is
> too elusive.

on the CEO and his or her problem or needs. Some accountability is silent, derived solely from peer pressure and the fact that the CEO will have to report on his or her status and progress toward his or her goal at the next meeting.

Another type is customized accountability, which essentially means you devise ways to hold yourself accountable for all progress, or lack thereof, in your ongoing effort to refine your focus and initiatives. Wendy's story illustrates the point.

News from the Trenches
At the first meeting of a new council, Wendy asked to be held accountable for achieving specific goals for her company. She requested that her peer council inquire about her status each month. She needed positive support to ensure she was working toward her goals. She also knew that was an area where she was weak. By listening and questioning, her council members could determine if she was making progress as planned. If not, her council members would point it out and help her get on track. Customized accountability within a peer group setting helped her grow as a business owner by encouraging her in the activities essential to her company's success.

Speakers or No Speakers

Peer-to-peer council meetings should be geared always toward the members, their businesses, and their goals and challenges. Because of possible distractions, I am reluctant to recommend inviting guest speakers to meetings. Finding one speaker whose words are relevant and meaningful to every CEO is rarely easy.

Typically, speakers present a concept or idea that's trending in the business world. That message rarely relates to an individual business's strategy, culture, or organizational structure. Usually a speaker presents a one-size-fits-all idea-of-the-day that a CEO should adapt to his or her business. More often than not, trendy messages and ideas set back the strategic process instead of moving it forward.

Change is Essential to Growth

We discussed change several times in this book, and for good reason. You join a peer advisory council to implement positive changes in your life and in your company. That's a key reason why the one-size-fits-all approach does not work for the peer-to-peer council meeting process—because each CEO has a different experience level. Each is seeking a unique sort of change for the better. Just as businesses require different strategic processes based on their success, CEOs use meeting processes that are indicative of each CEO's sophistication.

> The first step to growth is feeling uncomfortable.

As CEOs participate in meetings over the years, the meeting's structure should be adjusted to fit their growing business savvy. Changing the structure helps prevent the boredom and repetition caused by a predictable format. Once a year, moderators should consider presenting a new variation, process, or experience to the members. Regardless of what it is, it can help take the council members to the next level. For example, the evolution of My Transition™ changes as each council matures and evolves. CEOs and their businesses can only grow if their meeting process progresses with them.

The Evolution of Peer-to-Peer Councils

Councils that have met for years usually experience evolution. The processes used by mature councils differ vastly from the processes used by new or young councils. When a new member joins a council that has been in existence for years, it's important that the new member be quickly assimilated and educated to immediately benefit from participation without setting other members back. Valuable meeting time should never be used to initiate a new member into an existing council. The moderator or staff should bring the new member up to speed before his or her first meeting. Then time in the meeting can be used for the members to get to know each other on a level they are not familiar with. Charlie's story is instructive on this point.

News from the Trenches
Charlie has been the CEO of his electronic retail business for sixteen years. For the past eight years, he has been a member of the same peer advisory council, crediting it as central to his growth and success. He has accepted a handsome offer to buy his business and is looking forward to an early retirement. Charlie announced that with the sale of his business, he will be leaving his council.

Charlie's contribution to the council was significant, and the peer-to-peer council must find a replacement who will be a good match for the other council members in terms of level of growth. Ideally, the other members will take leadership in finding the best replacement by identifying who in the community might be a good candidate. It is a transitional stage for the council members, who are highly familiar with the history and unique challenges the other members face, as well as their personalities, strengths, and weaknesses. The goal is to ensure as seamless a transition as possible, so the new member should be brought up to speed on the progress, growth, challenges, and goals of the other members. By the time the new member attends the first meeting, he or she will have sufficient education and information to fill Charlie's spot and make a valuable and relevant contribution.

Finding the right peer advisory group may take some effort, but once you do, the benefits can be invaluable in terms of bolstering your personal and professional success. While you're not attending these meetings to make friends or network, you are going to form lasting bonds with peers you respect as you work together to help each other overcome challenges, capitalize on opportunities, solve problems, and inspire new ideas focused on enhanced business success.

> *I grew, developed and appreciated what others go through alone at the top and how we are not really alone together. It has proven to be an invaluable experience*
> *-Robert, Union Quarries, PA*

You'll find that the group will open up new vistas of thought you would not have otherwise seen. Often, a brilliant idea is just beneath the surface. Your peers can help you unearth ideas that can make all the difference for your business!

As an owner, you hold all the pressure and all the reward, literally. My friend and former partner Larry Linne often told the story of an employee that confessed to the owner that he had made a huge error or mistake that cost the company significant money. It was the employee's error, but it was ultimately the owner's consequence. As the business owner, you pay the price for everything. Each employee mistake comes out of your bottom line, not that employee's paycheck—literally. It is not uncommon for leaders to look at risk meaning something different from the average definition. For many, it means control and it means security. CEOs are the ones who determine their destiny; they literally impact the company's success or failure. As a business owner, you are the one that will determine and take all the risks and have all the pressure— the real risks, and the real pressure. And no real reward comes without that risk. I am sure you know that diamonds, one of the world's most prized gems, materialize only under extreme pressure. I equate that to being a business owner: no real reward materializes until you have experienced pressure to get there. Hence the "no pressure—no diamonds" analogy.

Pressure can be a positive for a CEO. Many thrive on pressure. They are challenged by it and gain energy from it. Then there are types of pressure not self-

> *"I can honestly say...the best investment in me in years."*
> -Amy, Credit Services, KS

induced that can be hard to manage and create stress. Regardless of the type of pressure, the point is you do not have to endure that pressure alone. The insights from involvement in a peer advisory council can determine the difference between wild success or below-average results.

In closing, let's recap what you need to figure out to see if a peer advisory council is right for you. Take a look at the following checklist to determine if you are ready to join a peer council.

- You are open to new ideas and perspectives.
- You realize you don't have all the answers.
- You realize there are things you don't know about business.
- You need unbiased feedback.
- You want to interact with successful peers on a deeper level.
- You want others to check your thinking, your blind spots.
- You feel lonely at the top.
- You need to take time out of the business to be more

strategic and proactive.

- You want to take your business to the next level.
- You can check your ego at the door.
- You are willing to help others who are willing to help you.
- You have business experiences to share.
- You desire a safe place to have candid conversations.
- You desire a sense of accountability.
- You want more peace of mind.

The best vision is insight. What does that mean? Often during marketing events to recruit peer council members, I ask business leaders to answer this question that I learned from participating as a client of Dan Sullivan's Strategic Coach: "If it were one year from today, what would make you happy with the progress you have made?" It is a question that generates clarity and immediate focus on what's important for now. Your answer is the one that we focus on with our members throughout the year. It's the one that as a CEO helps you to reach your vision, to bridge the gap between reality and vision. The answer is the one that shapes what you bring to your council to talk about, learn from their experiences, and gain insight into achieving results toward that answer.

> If it were one year from today, what would make you happy with the progress you have made?

In business, you can choose to go it alone or not, but I don't recommend the lone-wolf approach. In life, most people say their most memorable moments are ones that include others—a team, a coach, friends, or family. Rarely are they individual achievements with no one present. A peer council is your team, your place to share successes and challenges and be vulnerable.

One of my first strategic alliances was with Howard Bank's talented founder Mary Ann Scully. She once said that working together, we proved 2 + 2 can equal 7! Had I not partnered with Mary Ann, I would not have been nearly as successful early in my business. It proves going it alone is rarely as productive or rewarding.

You have now learned what a peer advisory council is, why participate, what the benefits are, and how to find a right-fit council for you. Why would any CEO of a financially stable company who wants to grow, whether personally in his or her role or grow the company, not join a peer advisory council when you can:

- bridge the gap between reality and the future more successfully
- hear real experiences that are relevant to your situation
- interact with peers and develop deep relationships that can last a lifetime
- make faster and better decisions
- become more proactive and less reactive
- save your company money
- become a better leader
- take action that creates greater results
- have access to resources locally from the recommendations of your peers
- gain insight into your blind spots through unbiased feedback
- be happier or spend more time on what you do best that brings greater value to the company
- be accountable
- have more energy and clarity

Being involved in a peer council can catapult you ahead faster, further, and smarter than you could ever do alone. You can have a phenomenal team of employees, but no team has your back more than your unbiased peer council. As your fellow business leaders, they are the ones who "get it."

I equate being in the right peer council to finding your dream team. Isn't it time to start your journey? You have the tools in this book to help you begin.

By being involved in a peer council, you will sit down in your council meeting to work "on" your business, you will speak up and be heard with your peers both in giving your insight and experiences and in receiving them, and the result is you will cash in on the ideas, perspectives, and feedback you receive.

Why wait to sit down, speak up, and cash in? Get started on the process today and chart a brighter future for you and your company!

Insights

- The ultimate peer council is one that you feel is your own.
- Members should get to approve new members joining.
- As an existing member, you want to be sure there is no conflict of interest with the new member.
- Members should feel leadership of the success and process of the council, not just the moderator.
- Matching CEOs to councils is like recruiters matching employees with companies.
- New members should receive orientation before the first meeting to not impede the council's progress.
- The right moderator does not attempt to impress, but as a result of doing his or her job well, he or she is impressive. He or she checks ego at the door.
- They have been trained on how to do this.
- The best moderator is skilled and trained in both business and in facilitating. He or she has:
  - a high degree of business acumen,
  - good listening skills,
  - checked ego,
  - desire to help others and contribute to their success,
  - diplomacy and tact, and

- ○ already achieved career success; he or she has nothing to prove.
- In the meetings, moderators facilitate. They do not coach, consult, or advise. They give their perspective and experience like the other members.
- A personal transition exercise before each meeting starts is vital.
- Take stock of your mind-set and let go of the day-to-day tactical and enter a strategic mind-set.
- Lack of process results in low value to the member. The meetings should not be rigid without flexibility, but meeting for the sake of meeting becomes unproductive quickly. Proven process and structure enable CEOs to learn and be open to knowing what is important to discuss.
- The level of accountability you want should match the level already determined by the existing council.
- A council's processes and structure should evolve ahead of the member's progress.
- Choose a council where you will benefit as well as benefit others. As you grow, the council overall needs to grow with a new structure that accommodates and challenges the needs of everyone.

Appendix

To better assist you in your search for the right peer advisory council, I've compiled several lists to help focus your thinking. Take a few minutes to look the material over. Pay special attention to the checklist you can use to determine what sort of group would be best for you. The material will help you see if you're ready to join a council. You'll see your options in terms of council types, and what questions to ask before you sign up.

A peer advisory council can change your entire outlook on your personal and business life. Rest assured, you'll find the right one if you take the time to look!

How do I know what questions to bring to my council for feedback, insights, and guidance?

Here are a few suggestions to get you started.
- What is causing frustration in your life today, whether personally or with the business?
- What area of the company is not performing?
- What is keeping you up at night?
- What problem exists that you are not addressing?
- What decision are you not making?
- What is causing the most customer dissatisfaction?
- What type of customer do you not have that you want?
- What market are you not in that you want to be?
- What division in the company is costing you money?
- What process is broken?
- What area is not as profitable as you'd like it to be?
- What are you not doing enough of in the business that you should be?
- What is holding you back from being the best CEO possible?
- What one thing would you like to change that would make the most positive impact to you and the company?
- What is causing you discomfort?

<u>Signs that you are ready to join a peer advisory council</u>

- ✓ You are open to new ideas and perspectives.
- ✓ You realize you don't have all the answers.
- ✓ You realize there are things you don't know about business.
- ✓ You are getting the same unsatisfactory results over and over.
- ✓ You want to interact with other peers on a deeper level.
- ✓ You feel lonely at the top as the owner.
- ✓ You need to take time out of the business to be more strategic and proactive.
- ✓ You want to take your business to the next level.
- ✓ You can check your ego at the door.
- ✓ You are willing to help others who are willing to help you.
- ✓ You have business experiences to share.
- ✓ You desire a safe place to have candid conversations.
- ✓ You are okay feeling uncomfortable at times, knowing it is for your own good.
- ✓ You want more peace of mind.

Checklist for Determining A Right-Fit Council

What stage is your business in today?

☐ Start-Up   ☐ Growth/Stability

☐ Entrepreneurial   ☐ Expanding

☐ Emerging   ☐ Maturity

What stage will your business be in three years from now?

☐ Start-Up   ☐ Growth/Stability

☐ Entrepreneurial   ☐ Expanding

☐ Emerging   ☐ Maturity

What is your budget?

☐ Low: pay nothing–$2,000/year

☐ Medium: $3,000–$15,000/year

☐ High: $20,000 or more/year

How much time can you commit?

☐ One day a month

☐ Four hours per month

☐ Quarterly meeting

☐ Annual meeting

As a business owner, what do you need to meet your business goals?

☐ Industry knowledge and expertise

☐ Peer influence

☐ Accountability

☐ Regular interaction

☐ Professional advice

☐ Knowledge about running a business

Do you want to own or plan the meeting?

☐ Yes   ☐ No

SIT DOWN! SPEAK UP! CASH IN!

Do you want a professional moderator for your meetings?

☐ Yes   ☐ No

How important is having a local meeting with peers who know about the local economy?

☐ Not important
☐ Somewhat important
☐ Very important

Are you seeking biased or unbiased perspective?

☐ Biased   ☐ Unbiased

Do you prefer an informal or formal meeting atmosphere and process?

☐ Informal   ☐ Formal

Are you willing to be open, candid, and vulnerable?

☐ Yes   ☐ No

Are you open to other ideas and perspectives?

☐ Yes   ☐ No

Are you willing to help others?

☐ Yes   ☐ No

Are you a good listener?

☐ Yes   ☐ No

Are you ready to take action?

☐ Yes   ☐ No

Are you willing to grow, both professionally and personally?

☐ Yes   ☐ No

Types of Boards

	Advisor Board	Friends & Family	Peer	Industry	Niche & Specialty	Own Advisor Board
Company Stage						
Entrepreneur	✓	✓	✓			
Emerging	✓	✓	✓			
Growth			✓	✓	✓	
Expanding			✓			
Mature			✓	✓	✓	✓
Time Commitment						
Self-Run	Yes	Yes	No	No	No	Yes
Moderator Run	No	No	Yes	Yes	Yes	No
$ Available Budget	Hourly by advisor	What you negotiate				Most investment
Needs						
Industry Knowledge		Maybe		✓	✓	✓
Peer Interaction	No	No	Yes	Yes	Yes	Yes
Accountability	Rare	No	Yes	Yes	Yes	Maybe
Meeting Frequency	Your decision	Your decision	Monthly	Quarterly or 2x a year	Monthly or 3–4x a year	3–4x a year
Biased vs. Unbiased	Biased	Biased	Unbiased	Unbiased	Unbiased	Varies
Fiduciary Responsibilities	No	No	No	No	No	Usually
Local Economy Knowledge	Yes	Usually	Yes	No	Yes	Depends

SIT DOWN! SPEAK UP! CASH IN!

Acknowledgements

To Sharon McManigle, my dear friend and colleague, for being the reason why this book got written. I would have never begun this journey without your unwavering encouragement, ideas, and confidence.

To Duane Carey, my marketing guru, for the inspiration to get it done and get it done right. His sense of humor, married with incredible marketing insight, helped me clarify the vision of this book.

To my very first peer council for your insights, friendship, and undying camaraderie: Dick Wallace, John Dini, Kevin Armstrong, Jackie Gernay, John Keener, Joe Zente, Bob French, Bernie Moscovitz, Mike Petrushka, and Bill Vettros.

To Vince Truant for being so gracious of your time and wisdom toward the vision of this concept. I'm eternally grateful for your involvement.

To Mary Ann Scully for believing in the peer advisory concept of partnering strategically to grow together. It was you who gave me the entry into banking alliances.

To Larry Linne, my business partner while at Intellectual Innovations. It was your sincere understanding and support of me that allowed me to follow my dream and what was in my heart. Our countless conversations on business-owner challenges helped me finesse the model of LXCouncil.

To Arthur for your advice, wisdom, and above all, humor in believing in building a legacy the right way.

About the Author

Tina Corner is the founder and CEO of LXCouncil, which is based in St. Petersburg, Florida. The company name is derived from Leadership Exchange, and it's quite fitting since the enterprise's core mission is to assist businesses in finding the right peer advisory groups comprised of noncompeting business leaders and leaders. These peer advisory groups offer participants an invaluable opportunity to exchange ideas  on how to grow their companies, chart a path to enhanced success, and learn how to deal with business problems more effectively.

Tina's vast experience in working with peer advisory councils goes back to when she owned a franchise of The Alternative Board. The firm specialized in the development of peer advisory groups for business leaders. After nearly 10,000 hours spent successfully developing peer- to-peer councils under the TAB umbrella, Tina sold her franchise in 2012. At the time, it was the fastest-launched franchise in TAB history. Tina's franchise membership grew to include nearly fifty Maryland companies in less than two years and nearly eighty upon her exit, making her the largest single-owner peer board franchisee in the world.

Tina was recently president at Intellectual Innovations, LLC, where she managed the intellectual property and implemented the executive training of the Noise Reduction SystemTM (NRS), which is the proprietary system developed from the book Make the Noise Go Away by Larry G. Linne. The training program is offered through universities and colleges, associations and partners located nationally and internationally. Now Intellectual Innovations is a strategic partner with LXCouncil, providing proprietary tools for its members.

Tina has more than twenty years of experience in senior executive positions in every size company from start-ups to a multibillion-dollar global telecom organization with P&L responsibility for over $1.2 billion and 1,300 employees.

She is a graduate of Harvard Business School's Program for Management Development, has a BS in marketing and business logistics from the University of Missouri, and is certified in DISC and PIAV behavior assessments.

To learn more about Tina and her company and about how a peer advisory council could help you and your business, visit www.LXCouncil.com or call 410-970-4771.